What others Are Saying About Ou

ISP® Certification The Industrial Security Professional Exam Manual

"Written by a security consultant with twenty-two years of experience in military intelligence, contracting and security, ISP Certification: The Industrial Security Professional Exam Manual is an instructional resource created to provide career security specialists with what they need to know to protect our nation's secrets. The text offers practical advice for security professionals and a working understanding of the NISPOM and Presidential Executive Orders implementing the National Industrial Security Program, but the heart of ISP Certification is its four practice tests designed to probe the depths of one's knowledge. An absolute "must-have" for anyone in federal positions requiring a thorough knowledge of security procedures, and highly recommended for the libraries of federal agencies." Midwest Book Review

"Right on target! Jeffrey Bennett's exam manual is the perfect supplement to the NISPOM for anyone preparing to take the Industrial Security Professional certification exam. The approach is clear and easy to use. It's definitely worth the price and more." William H. Henderson, author, Security Clearance Manual

"After receiving this book, I quickly skimmed through it prior to sitting down for a close study. My initial reaction was to wonder just how much information I could learn based on the fact that most of the book was dedicated to practice tests. When I finally took the time to sit down and read it, I was surprised at just how much information it contains. The book tells you how to prepare, to include learning all security disciplines, how to manage your time, and how to study the NISPOM. The practice tests are a great opportunity to time yourself, and help to identify areas of weakness. I truly recommend this book for anyone considering the ISP Certification… it is a great tool to have!"

"As most others I am a seasoned FSO. However, based on research I did, once I decided to take the ISP Exam I quickly learned to not take it cold. I got my workbook from NCMS and researched what other tools are out there to better help prepare me for the exam. I quickly discovered Mr. Bennett's ISP certification manual and after reading the overwhelmingly positive reviews I knew this would be well worth the money! "

"I've ordered a few of your products, to include the ISP manual and flash cards. I wanted you to know that I took the ISP exam this morning and passed! Your products were very helpful."

"I could not have attained a high score on the ISP exam without your study materials. The study materials you provided helped me prepare for this certification. I am very happy to be a part of this elite group of professionals."

"I could not have attained a high score on the ISP exam without your study materials. The study materials you provided helped me prepare for this certification. I am very happy to be a part of this elite group of professionals." Tony Cirafice, ISP Security Specialist

"The study guide has helped keep me up to date on the NISPOM." Kenneth Chaney, ISP, GA

"You have captivated the reader's interest!! Throughout the reading, you continue to address educational encouragement, experience and networking. The emphasis on mentoring just goes to show you how important it is to have support of your peers. Many who may be apprehensive about taking the exam, probably feel like they are all alone and no one is there to lean on. This book is an amazing tool to help guide and support those interested in rising to the next level. This book supports the certification's demonstration of willingness for self-improvement and dedication to the profession." Deb Jaramillo, ASIS North AL Chapter Secretary

"As a seasoned security professional, I found the Industrial Security Professional Exam Manual to be very clear, brief and concise. The ISP manual is a must read for anyone anticipating taking the ISP exam. Whether you are a seasoned security professional or a newbie to the world of security, this book is a keeper. Thank you for putting out such a Great Book ." Diane Griffin, President/CEO, Security First & Associates LLC

"Like many seasoned industrial security representatives, I feel like I know it all. I have been in this industry almost 25 years; I know where to look for answers, and I have my contacts. But one day it occurred to me just how much has changed during my career - enter the Internet, enter computer based training, enter instant security clearances (Interims), enter the JPAS/e-QIP interface, enter diminished contact with my cleared employees and visitors. Admitting that the contact with my cleared employees is not as intimate as it used to have to be, somehow I felt that I was losing touch with my own skill set because of it. You should consider buying the ISP Certification - The Industrial Security Professional Exam Manual, and spend 30 minutes with it each evening after work. Reinvigorate yourself. Give your imagination and professional growth some quiet stimulation. Remember. Refresh yourself. The best security education dollar you can spend, and not even leave home." Lisa Doman, Sierra Vista, AZ

"Jeff provides a paramount service with his book that assists in taking the ISP test. He gives insight into what is needed to help you be certified in the security industry today. Jeff's dedication and attention to detail is second to none and I highly recommend him on a professional level." Kenneth Wontz, President. Trinity Security Consultants, VA

DOD Security Clearances and Contracts Guidebook

"Jeffrey Bennett's comprehensive guide gives defense contractors all the information they need to establish and maintain a successful security program. He pulls together information from Presidential Executive Orders and regulations from numerous government agencies. Readers will learn how to appoint and train a facility security officer, navigate the security clearance process, win contracts dealing with classified information, and how to secure and protect that information."

"An excellent book for companies trying to get into the world of classified government contracts. It is a great starting point for new Facility Security Officers, telling them what they need to know in order to be successful at their job."

How to Get U.S. Government Contracts and Classified Work

"Loaded with insightful information about all of the concerns and roadblocks most small businesses have to get into the Defense industry. A must-have for new defense businesses and seasoned companies looking to improve their operations and security procedures."

"This book was extremely helpful and provides detailed information on how to get government contracts and classified work. It is a must for anyone wanting to get into government contracting. Jeff Bennett is knowledgeable on the topic and an expert. I highly recommend his book."

"With Jeff's bevy of knowledge and insight into DOD you are guaranteed to grow your book of business with the government. A must read for people who want to understand this landscape."

Insider's Guide to Security Clearances

"Having been tasked with the mission to research all that I could about Security Clearances and the Facility Security Officer (FSO) position at a government contracting firm, it was difficult to find resources on the topic that were available for the up-and-coming FSO. In this book, Mr. Bennett gives clear and concise answers to help guide the way for those that haven't been in the industry for long or at all. And with the Kindle edition, it was easy to have the book with me for reference whenever I needed help with knowing which forms to use, what acronyms stand for, and what is the next step in the Security Clearance process."

"The book is great-- cuts to the point on how to get started in this business. Succinctly describes what you need to do to get your business set up to work on clearance contracts. Gives you helpful links, and does a fairly good job at listing out the "to-do's".

"Excellent for Defense professionals who want to understand and simplify the typically confusing landscape of security clearances. Jeff really knows his stuff and makes it very digestible to keep yourself safe and compliant!"

A special word of thanks and a favor to ask

Thank you for buying my book. I really appreciate you being a reader and hope you find it helpful. If you have any questions, please feel free to contact me.

I would really love to hear your feedback and your input would help to make the next version of this book and my future books better. Please leave a helpful review, where you purchased your book, of what you thought of it.

I would also ask that you let a friend know about the book as well. Thanks so much and best of success to you!!

Jeffrey W. Bennett

Sign up for our reader newsletter:
https://www.redbikepublishing.com/contact

For more information on cleared defense contracting, security clearances, and training, check out our video.
https://www.redbikepublishing.com/security/

We also have cleared contractor, security clearance and National Industrial Security Program Operating Manual (NISPOM) training at Bennett Institute that could compliment your certification studies.

https://www.bennettinstitute.com

ISP® and ISOC Master Exam Prep
Learn Faster, Retain More, Pass the Exam

For 32 CFR Part 117

ISP® and ISOC Master Exam Prep
Learn Faster, Retain More, Pass the Exam

For 32 CFR Part 117

Jeffrey W. Bennett, ISOC, ISP®, SAPPC, SFPC

www.redbikepublishing.com

ISP® and ISOC Master Exam Prep - Learn Faster, Retain More, Pass the Exam For 32 CFR Part 117

Published by: Red Bike Publishing www.redbikepublishing.com

Published in the United States of America
www.redbikepublishing.com

ISBN: 978-1-936800-41-4
LCCN: 2022934905

About the Author

Jeffrey W. Bennett, ISOC, ISP®, SAPPC, SFPC is a security expert with experience in the Army, U.S. Government and as a Facility Security Officer (FSO). He holds ISP® certificate number 117. Jeff developed this study manual to help motivate his peers and offer them an opportunity to take practice tests.

Jeff is enthusiastic about protecting our nation's secrets. He believes that integrity, influence and credibility are paramount qualities required of security professionals. His primary goal is to show security specialists how to bring about security awareness, build influence within the organization and to make a difference where they work.

Jeff advises on national security issues and is a former Army officer who has served in military intelligence, logistics and speaks three languages. He has an MBA from Columbia College and a Master's Degree in Acquisitions and Procurement Management from Webster University. A teacher at heart, he is board certified to protect classified information. He speaks, writes and provides products to help professionals better protect sensitive and classified information. This book provides security education and helps security specialists earn their certification. Additionally, Jeff is the author of *How to Get U.S. Government Contracts and Classified Work, Insider's Guide to Security Clearances, Get Rich in a Niche-Insider's Guide to Self-Publishing* and several novels. Jeff is a featured speaker in many venues including a presenter at the University of Alabama in Huntsville.

To find out more about the author, visit: www.redbikepublishing.com and his blog at http://dodsecurity.blogspot.com.

About Red Bike Publishing, LLC

Our company is registered as a government contractor with the CCR and VetBiz (DUNS 826859691). Specifically we are a service disabled veteran owned small business. Our mission is to help you accomplish yours. Smart businesses know that rather than trying to focus on everything at once they should devote resources to more effectively executing their mission. Red Bike Publishing is here to provide value added writing and security services to include NISPOM, ITAR, ISP® Certification Study Tips, security awareness training resources, and safe magnets.

See more at www.redbikepublishing.com.

A Note to the Reader

Congratulations on buying this book. You have just taken the first step to improving your understanding of certification testing. Inside you'll discover techniques and methodologies you need to develop or augment an existing study program. In fact, I want you to read the first two chapters today so that you can get a good foundation that you will be able to apply immediately.

I want to help you develop confidence to take the test. Many people have let fear of failure, lack of understanding, and lack of peer support keep them from registering for certification. To to this, I have written this book to bring you beyond just going through the study or test prep motions. This book covers information from Presidential Executive Orders and the NISPOM that you need to know to prepare for and pass the exams.

You know how everyone recommends becoming certified, but don't explain well how to do it? I wrote this book to help security professionals understand the National Industrial Security Program Operating Manual (NISPOM) and apply knowledge to simulated test environments found in the ISP® and ISOC certifications.

Being technically proficient is great, but becoming certified gets you noticed. This book helps you do that. For those who desire to supplement test preparation, this book will show you how to do so. It unravels the web of requirements and assists with how to apply the NISPOM so you can confidently approach the exam.

The security industry is booming and defense industry security specialists are benefiting. Departments of Defense, Department of Energy, the Nuclear Regulatory Commission, Central Intelligence Agency, and many other Federal and supporting contractors are in great need of experienced and qualified security specialists, managers and Facility Security Officers. As the industry becomes more demanding and positions more competitive, today's security specialists need to be on top of their game.

This may be helpful as a supplement to certification studies. At the very least, it can prepare professionals to better protect classified information under their care. I believe the certification process is just a stepping stone and not an end to a means. In fact, it's just part of a plan to help you become more influential. Being technically proficient is great, but building influence and commanding respect is more important. This book will help you make the move from being an administrator to becoming the "go to" security manager.

The opening chapters demonstrate the importance of building networks, getting professional and academic education, and finding mentors. Credibility is the key to influence and learning from others in the industry helps you build confidence in your decisions and capabilities. I also provide ideas for those of you who perform very few of the security functions identified in NISPOM. Our helpful hints increase experience and confidence and provide ideas for hands on training. You can also join our newsletter for updates, security awareness ideas, and NISPOM topics. Register for our newsletter, full of NISPOM ideas at https://www.redbikepublishing.com

Dedication

This book is dedicated to the men and women of all vocations and walks of life who defend our country and protect our nation's secrets.

Acknowledgement

None of this would have been possible without the loving support of my family. You have so willingly provided encouragement while understanding my need to write this book. To my colleagues Polly Rupe, ISP® and Jackie Tippins, ISP®, and the many, many FSOs and security specialists who choose to remain unnamed, thanks for the technical editing, advice, and encouragement. I would also like to thank Shama Patel for her social media support and editing services. You can reach her at Evening Light Designs, LLC.

https://www.eveninglightdesigns.com

Disclaimer

This book is designed to give practice questions to those who are eligible to take the certifications such as the ISP® and Security Professional Education Development (SPēD) certifications, specifically the ISOC. I have written this book with the understanding that it will assist with exam studies, but should not to be used as a standalone product. Our intention is to compliment career experience and NISPOM guidance.

All security and compliance related issues that an organization may face should be pursued with the Cognizant Security Agency, Government Contracting Activity or other applicable federal agencies and legal activities. This book is meant to compliment the federal regulations and executive orders bringing about the NISP. It is also designed to help the reader draw from experience and suggests ways to study for and take certification exams. Those who are new to the field can use this as a study guide. However, in all cases this is not a guaranteed single source option for passing the exam. My intent is to present practice questions to prepare you for the test experience and not to suggest actual questions that may be found in any certification exam. I do not know what those actual questions may be.

As an ISP® and SPēD certified author, I have made every effort to make this manual as accurate and complete as possible. Some of the most experienced Facility Security Officers and ISP®s in the business have reviewed and edited this product.

Table of Contents

CHAPTER 1-WHY YOU SHOULD GET A CERTIFICATION

Thanks again for buying this book. I am so glad you did and wish you well in your journey to become and ISP® and ISOC certified professional. Security professionals who either desire certification or have responsibility of the careers of those who do, don't always know where to go to find information on what might be expected of them. Some might form study groups, take online training, find a mentor, but still lack actual practice questions focused on NISPOM guidance.

I began writing this book while preparing for the ISP® Certification exam. I would study sections of NISPOM, rehearsing chapter and subchapter topics, writing practice questions, performing self-inspections, and interviewing ISP®s. Since most people I spoke with stated the biggest obstacle was running out of time, I wanted to answer the question: "How do I complete a 110 question open book test about the NISPOM during a 120 minute session?".

I realized that memorization would not be a good method for this test. More likely, I needed to consider the NISPOM structure and how to apply it. The NISPOM is an administrative guidance document describing what should be done to protect classified information, but not how to do it. I expected that if I studied where to find answers and how to apply the NISPOM topically, I could complete the test in enough time to check my work.

That's exactly what happened. Using information I provide in this book, I completed the test in 90 minutes; 30 minutes to spare. I realized that my study method had proven successful and that I could teach it to others.

There is study material available at NCMS and CDSE for the ISP® and ISOC preparation. This book is intended to augment that study material and provide proven study methodology to help you better understand the NISPOM and how to apply it. You will have more confidence in your ability to answer all test questions in the amount of time provided. The following chapters will help you understand the NISPOM and give you access to four full length practice tests and many essay questions. So, let's get started.

The National Industrial Security Program

On Friday January 8, 1993, the President of the United States signed Executive Order (EO) 12829, establishing the National Industrial Security Program (NISP). The program is commonly referred to as the NISP and is an acronym with which those working with classified contracts should become familiar. The NISP gives excellent guidance, training and directions with which industrial security professionals can better protect classified information. It also creates agencies that have oversight of contractors performing on classified contracts.

According to the EO, the program's purpose is to safeguard classified information that has been or may be released to…"current, prospective, or former contractors, licensees, or grantees of United States agencies". It is also designed to provide for the protection of classified material as outlined in EO 12958 and the Atomic Energy Act of 1954, as amended.

The President also requires that the Secretary of Defense consult with agencies and work with the Secretary of Energy, the Nuclear Regulatory Commission, and the Director of Central Intelligence to issue and maintain the National Industrial Security Program Manual (NISPOM).

The ISP®

The Industrial Security Professional (ISP®) Certification is sponsored by NCMS (Society of Industrial Security Professionals), a professional organization of industrial security[1] members specializing in protecting classified information. This group of professionals works in an industry operating under the NISP. To achieve the goal of providing education and professionalism, NCMS has developed the ISP® Certification. The ISP® bearer demonstrates a high level of knowledge in topics involving safeguarding classified information. The certification is based on the NISPOM but also covers elective topics. However, I recommend a good foundation in NISPOM as adequate to pass the exam without having to study the elective topics.

As with most professional certifications, earning the ISP® certification is recognized as a major accomplishment. The ISP® does indeed distinguish the bearer from those not certified and there is emphasis within NCMS to elect ISP® Certified national and local chapter leaders. Because of the intense study involved, the certification demonstrates willingness for self-improvement and dedication to the profession. The ISP® also communicates to management that the professional is committed to the business, the industry, and the furtherance of national security. Employees with certifications help put their companies in a stronger negotiation position while bidding on contracts and lend credibility to relationships with the oversight office, DCSA. Most of all, it gives the recipient confidence in the knowledge base and the ability to apply the knowledge to make vital decisions.

As this certification program evolves, more and more employers will recognize the certified industrial security professional during job interviews. In addition, the ISP® certification could make the difference between which applicant gets the Facility Security Officer job offer and which security administrator gets the promotion.

A Note to Military and Government Employee Security Specialists

There are several reasons for those working in government and the military to achieve certification. One of which allows security managers to take advantage of opportunities offered in the recent Presidential Executive Order: National Security Professional Development. The Executive order states: "In order to enhance the national security of the United States…it is the policy of the United States to promote the education, training, and experience of current and future professionals in national security positions (security professionals)…".

The national strategy identified in the Executive Order provides a plan to give security professionals access to education and training designed to increase their professional experience. This creates a more effective body of professionals dedicated to protecting our nation's secrets.

The NISPOM may not be familiar to you, but the security functions identified within should be. The NISPOM is the government contractor's guidance from DoD on how to receive, process, and distribute classified information. It demonstrates how to mark, document, store, disseminate, and destroy classified information as well as how to set up classified computing. If in the course of your duties you have or expect to have a contractual classified agreement with a member of U.S. industry or have oversight of those who do, you should be familiar with their requirements as identified in the NISPOM.

Currently, the Department of the Defense offers SPēD certification. The SPēD certified security manager can demonstrate the knowledge and skills to perform critical tasks as well as relate well with civilian counterpart requirements. Most of all, it gives the bearer confidence in their ability to apply their knowledge. As this certification program evolves, it is expected that more and more employers will require the certification.

---

1 For the purpose of this book, Industrial Security refers to that portion of information security concerned with the protection of classified information in the custody of U.S. industry. This is a National Industrial Security Program Operating Manual (NISPOM) term that should not be confused with the same terminology used in other security fields.

Industrial Security Oversight Certification (ISOC)

DoD personnel, federal employees or contractors assigned to a security position and employed by an agency accepted for participation in the SPēD Certification Program are eligible for the certification. It's a good idea to contact your SPēD Certification Program Component Service Representative (CSR) if you have questions about your eligibility (https://www.cdse.edu/certification/sped_contact.html).

ISOC Area of Expertise

The Industrial Security Oversight Certification (ISOC) assessment measures your understanding of industrial security skills in implementing the NISP and its manual, the NISPOM. This includes assessing the tester's application of other industrial security functions, such as facility security and conducting facility surveys and inspections.

It's possible that you may be actively engaged in only one or two of the core security disciplines (i.e., information, personnel, physical, industrial, or general security). However, for future career opportunities (and test taking) it is important to demonstrate a fundamental knowledge across the core disciplines and the ability to perform industrial security oversight functions. For this reason, we have included all areas in this study guide. The ISOC is not only valuable to you as your career advances; it also strengthens the confidence the DoD has in your specialized knowledge in industrial security oversight.

Understanding the test tips will reduce frustration and prepare you for the actual test. I have attempted to simulate the test environment through this book and on the online exam @ https://www.classmarker.com/online-test/start/?quiz=jdm5dbdb6cb9c613. If you understand the tips, then you can approach the test properly. Where the ISP® test focuses on selecting the correct multiple-choice answer, the ISOC focuses on what the tasks are and how to perform them. Though this study guide provides multiple-choice answers, the reader should ask application questions and rehearse their answers instead of selecting the best of the multiple-choice answers. The best approach to this study guide is to address the practice tests as provided and then go back through answer the questions as essay questions. To get you started, we have included a few essay style questions in Appendix A.

While the ISP® certification exam is open book, the ISOC is not. However, the study material is the same and an understanding of NISPOM is necessary to pass the exam. I would also argue that the NISPOM is the primary document for ISOC study. The best study guide and resources for ISOC can be found at the CDSE website provided earlier. If you are eligible to take the ISOC, then you will have access to the website. Study the material focusing on topics that make up the largest volume of the certification exam.

Next, use this study manual to practice additional questions in a simulated test environment. Using this multiple question study aid will help reinforce and expand knowledge of the NISPOM to assist the test taker with confidence of NISPOM knowledge and developing test taking confidence. The test taker should be familiar with the test scope and know the answers. Understanding the test topic concepts and regular practice is key and this book provides a way to address the test successfully.

Commit

There are many reasons to step out and get certified. From career development to the satisfaction of accomplishment and prestige, certification fulfills many desires and goals. However, there may be many more excuses not to take a certification exam. Some excuses include the expense, time involved, embarrassment of failure, and just plain fear. If you follow the principles set forth in this book you will improve your chances of passing, creating your professional legacy, improving your standing, increasing your salary, and rising to the top in your chosen field.

CHAPTER 2 WHAT CERTIFICATION IS NOT

I had a boss who liked to say that a degree and a quarter will get you a cup of coffee and she was absolutely right. In comparison, certification is a measurement of your knowledge...period. Many people can study, take a test and earn a certificate. The number of unemployed college graduates demonstrates that credentials alone do not guarantee success at any level. However, those who have applied themselves to good work ethic, moral uprightness, and the discipline of marrying their knowledge with practical application, move on to bigger and better things. In the case of certification, the benefits are only manifested with demonstrated ability and technical knowledge.

Certification is not the end, but part of the certified professional's journey. It is as vital to career development as is the training offered by government organizations, university, management seminars, and annual inspections. Importantly, the professional also understands that just because they earn a degree or certification does not mean automatic raises and promotions. The raises and promotions are a result of application of education, work ethic, ability to achieve, certifications, and demonstrated ability to perform. It's part of the whole package. For example, one should never say, "I'll take the certification exam to get that raise or promotion. This certification will prove I am ready". Instead, the professional would say, "Because I am knowledgeable in my field and I have demonstrated my ability, I will become certified to further demonstrate my commitment, professionalism, credibility, and technical competence". One should not expect to earn great things by passing a test. Be prepared to demonstrate the knowledge.

If you have ambitions for higher positions in security, becoming a leader, or if you would like to increase your NISPOM knowledge, study. Let the study preparation be part of your overall goal. This should be a stepping stone amongst others in a path to your destination.

Goals should be outlined and identified with action steps. For example, to become an expert in the field or build credibility as a Facility Security Officer (FSO) or security specialist it may prove beneficial to get an MBA, publish articles, earn certification, and speak at events. In the goals outline list the goal on top and the action steps under the goal. If you want to earn certification, that would be the goal. Joining study groups, downloading resources, reading the NISPOM and taking on NISPOM based projects would be the steps.

Goal	Step 1	Step 2	Step 3	Step 4	Step 5
Security Certification (ISP® ISOC)	Register for exam (countdown to test)	Get copy of NISPOM	Seek study material such as online training, books, libraries, etc.	Find mentor	Form study group
	Resources	**Resources**	**Resources**	**Resources**	**Resources**
	ISP® NCMS	DCSA Website	NCMS website	NCMS mentor program	Local Network
	ISOC CDSE	redbikepublishing.com	CDSE website	Security specialists in network	
			bennettinstitute.com		
			redbikepublishing.com		

Furthermore, industrial security leaders learn to be technically, politically, and academically savvy. They are not looking for a magic bullet to help them wake up in the position, they are living in such a way to be worthy of the title (demonstrated knowledge) before the event. In other words, they are being successful before the reward is given.

Getting Started

Since certification is a stepping stone toward your career success, it would make sense to chart a path leading to the test event. Developing a written plan is critical, helps maintain focus and keeps test anxiety at bay. It's easy to say, "next year I'll take the test." The tough part is maintaining the focus and discipline to get there.

If your plan calls for studying NISPOM 20 minutes a day, joining a study group, and personally conducting the 27 item *Self-Inspection Handbook for NISP Contractors*, you project an accurate time line from registration to test. These goals also keep you from rushing the time line and taking the test before you are ready.

Develop a Plan

The first step is to register for the exam. This registration process ensures that you meet qualifications and are eligible to take the exam. Additionally, registering for the exam commits you to the event. If you wait until you are ready to take the exam, you may never feel "ready". The added pressure of an actual date can prove motivating. In most cases, you can register and schedule a test date up to one year in advance.

Next, get a copy of the NISPOM online or for a printed version, go to www.redbikepublishing.com and seek out our NISPOM, and related books and training. Read the NISPOM over a period of time. Don't try to cram the entire manual in all at once as you risk losing that knowledge within minutes of testing. Remember, we are going for a lifestyle and professional shake up. What we do in preparation for certification must stick with us throughout our careers. The purpose of this guide is not only to help you pass the test, but to become proficient, implement effective programs and increase your ability to protect our nation's assets.

It is not necessary to memorize the NISPOM, just become familiar with where to find the information in the performance of your duties. You need to not only be able to access information for your job, but you need to know how to find it fast to be able to answer 110 questions in two hours. Become familiar with the content of each chapter to answer the following questions:

What do chapters cover? What categories do paragraphs and sections explain? How does the NISPOM sections apply to your craft? Make it part of your daily regimen to relate the chapter to the subject. For example, know that FSO reporting and eligibility requirements are found in chapter one, facility clearances are found in chapter two, and computer security is found in chapter eight.

For online test taking purposes, prepare a folder that you can easily access for study and testing. One incredible tool is the before mentioned electronic NISPOM. Some certification exams use searchable references. When taking the computer exam you can search answers by topic. This requires a great deal of practice in choosing the right keyword. The test questions in the book can give you the practice necessary to help prepare

Seek additional study resources. You should primarily start with the organizations who oversee or facilitate the certification. For the ISP®, it's the NCMS. For the ISOC, it's CDSE. Visit their websites and become familiar with their training available. I also recommend books about the NISP such as my book *How to Get U.S. Government Contracts and Classified* work which is a chapter by chapter walk through of the NISPOM and how to apply it. Additionally, each chapter has review questions that you can answer on how to apply the NISPOM lessons. Next, use this book to supplement that training with practice tests.

Find a mentor. Humans are meant to be part of a team. We work best when we work together. Loads are carried farther, work levels are reduced significantly, and costs have less impact. You may already work within a large security team. However, I recommend that you find a mentor who will challenge you to step outside of your organization and comfort zone. This mentor should be in the security business, and working under the NISP.

A mentor can share experiences with you. They will have demonstrated expertise in their fields, have a good reputation within the industry and will know how to direct you to answer NISPOM or elective area subject matter questions. Your mentor should be a cheerleader who knows your goals and would appreciate seeing you reach success. They will call on you to check progress or meet with you for questions. This relationship will reach beyond the certification goal as mentors coach you through life. This person does not badmouth others or talk you out of your goals; nobody has time for that.

For additional support, consider joining or starting a study group. It's good to be accountable to both a mentor and a peer group. You may find that there are many local security specialists who would love to join you in your goals. If no one is local, consider using available resources to start web conferences or other online study platforms.

Education

This study guide can assist you with the electronic version of the test. Also, be sure to obtain hard copy or electronic versions of the SF86, DD Form 254, SF 312, data base user manuals, and other resources helpful to your profession. You may find many questions from the exam addressed to those resources.

Simply use this manual to simulate the test and practice searching the answers using the same NISPOM you will use during the exam. Select the search function in the Adobe Acrobat NISPOM.

A great place to practice additional NISPOM specific subject online exams is the Defense Counterintelligence and Security Agency (DCSA). There you can register for an account from the website at www.dcsa.mil. Set up an account to access their online training resources. The DCSA has courses with tests that will help prepare you to take lengthy online exams. The tests and courses are based on the NISPOM and studying them will greatly increase your professional knowledge.

Experience

Another stone on your path is to work on different security projects. You can do this internally or outside of your company. For example, if you are working in personnel security and your primary function is to request security clearances, volunteer to learn about other security functions like classified contract management. Subcontracting, performance of classified work, facility and personnel clearance directives are driven by the DD Form 254. Stepping into this new world will give insight into personnel security functions and offer a broader perspective of security duties necessary. This is beneficial for further career development and familiarization with ISP® exam topics.

Consider volunteering to conduct some of the tasks found in *Self-Inspection Handbook for NISP Contractors.* This will give you an opportunity to study requirements, evaluate progress, make decisions, correct problems, and advise in all areas of security. If you want to separate yourself from the mediocre performers, step out and assume the role. You will amaze yourself with the exponentially increasing skills developed from interaction with different security areas while serving as a company "consultant" or self-review leader.

If you are really feeling adventurous, put together a self-review team. As the leader, you can meet regularly with your team to discuss findings, develop corrective courses of action, brief results, and recommend solutions. In this leadership capacity, you will accelerate your learning curve. Other professionals will soon approach you for solutions, thus improving your self confidence and credibility.

This is a great time to dive into the world of physical security. You can interact with security guards and work with them as they conduct their routes and questions concerning NISPOM requirements. Volunteer to be on call. There is nothing like being the "go to" person at 2:00 am while responding to alarms. Such situations require study of policies and NISPOM requirements and ability to react to stressful events.

If your mission makes it possible, step into new opportunities with certifying closed areas and vaults. It is one thing to read about requirements in the NISPOM and quite another to personally go through the checklists. This will prepare you for questions concerning false ceilings, construction requirements,and intrusion detection systems. The point is to get involved with all aspects of security and away from your comfort zone. Besides becoming certification worthy, you may find yourself rewarded in other ways.

Study Groups

There are many ways to form a study group. As mentioned earlier, humans are made for companionship and teamwork. Study groups facilitate learning as everyone shares experiences and helps each other find answers. You will also be able to hold each other accountable, write practice tests, and encourage one another. Concentrate on studying for the exam and make it the primary focus. Write a study plan, keep an agenda and assign someone in the group responsible for enforcing the rules and keeping focus.

In keeping with the theme of certification being part of career development, study groups offer other benefits such as instant networking. There, you may find an audience of security professionals with a wide range of expertise and have many experiences that they would love to share. The benefit of being in a network is greater than the amount of the members. At some point in your career (more often than not) you may find that you may have questions or concerns about company security policies and how they support the NISPOM. Would it not be nice to have someone to bring those concerns to who will give sound advice with no penalties? Also, guess where you might be able to find one of your mentors?

As you continue to improve your skills, take a moment to visualize what certification will bring to your career. Ask yourself how it will distinguish you from your peers. You may be inspired to uphold the ethical standards of the certification. You may be motivated by having to work to continuously learn, publish, teach, and encourage keeping your certification current. Perhaps you will be inspired by the prestige and credibility the certification brings to you and your profession. Perhaps you want the title to put in your business card, or the certificate for your wall. Whatever the motivation, use it to propel yourself toward the goal of earning your next certification.

Additional Resources

Be sure to check out the last few pages of this book for additional resources to assist you with your studies. These references include, the NISPOM, books and training about NISPOM, and other great resources to augment your studies.

CHAPTER 3 THE NISPOM

One last thing before we get started on practice questions. I recommend spending some time getting to know the NISPOM. Don't rely on your ability to answer these questions as they may or may not be on the test. Memorizing these questions should not be a milestone to measure your success. You can measure your success as your ability to answer these practice questions primarily because you know how to find them in NISPOM (ISP® exam) or you understand how to apply NISPOM (ISOC exam).

The NISPOM is the foundational study resource both exams are tied to. Spend your time studying this document since up to 90% of test questions are found there. Study the NISPOM topically (training, reporting, security clearance, storage, etc) and you will have a better understanding of both where to find the answers and how to apply them. For example, if the question asks which agency has oversight of NISPOM, you would understand that the answer can be found in NISPOM 32 CFR Part 117.2. For ISP® candidates, that means you can go to 117.1 and search. For ISOC candidates, you would understand that 117.2 discusses responsibilities of the DoD, and other agency head. From there, you should be able to confidently answer an essay question. In other words, you will be able to use this information to reasonably deduct the correct answer. So, instead of just charging through the questions, dedicate time to study the NISPOM topically and use the sample test questions to reinforce your knowledge.

So, on to the NISPOM.

The NISPOM provides restrictions, rules, guidelines, and procedures for preventing unauthorized disclosure of classified material; it is the primary regulatory reference for performing industrial security. The NISPOM applies to authorized users of classified information and equips those working on classified contracts with the critical instruction on how to implement the NISP in their organizations. It is up to the contractor and the oversight agency to work together to provide accurate interpretation of the guidelines to the specific classified contract requirements. It is this interpretation that the oversight agency will use while conducting annual security reviews.

The Secretary of Defense and the other identified agencies apply the concept of Risk Management while implementing the NISPOM. There are three factors necessary in determining risk. The first is the level of damage to national security that could be reasonably expected to result from unauthorized disclosure of classified material. It is important to know that the NISPOM provides explicit guidance to user agencies on how to identify and protect classified items at all levels.

Though the NISPOM provides guidance, it doesn't tell you how to execute. It is up to you to determine how to apply it for test purposes. In real life, the Facility Security Officer (FSO) interprets the NISPOM and applies it to the Cleared Defense Contractor (CDC). The cognizant security agency (for the DoD it is Defense Counterintelligence and Security (DCSA)). Success depends on a mutual working relationship between the contractor and the government entity. The intent of the NISPOM isn't to burden the company, but to help it execute a successful security program. The 32 CFR Part 117 NISPOM is broken down into paragraphs, each having a specific topic.

The NISPOM is the industrial security professional's go to source for conducting the business of protecting our nation's resources. Learning or becoming familiar with chapter contents will assist the FSO with establishing a security program, assist oversight organizations with what to inspect, and assists certification exam subjects with where to find answers and helps formulate the answers. Far greater in context, the NISPOM is to be used as a guide that can only help improve national security with a good and positive agency/industry working model.

The NISPOM sets the rules and the government/industry relationship demonstrates how to implement the NISP. The designated FSO develops the skills to run the cleared defense contractor's security program. That means knowing where to find the answers and develop effective solutions. This means knowing how to interpret the NISPOM and explain it to business units, marketing, contracts, and the executive staff. Learn their language and let them know how you contribute to their business success. The security specialist's job is to have NISPOM make sense, and as the ISP® or ISOC certification exam participant, you should also learn it well.

I understand taking such a certification endeavor is scary. Most will not certify only because they fear failure or fear test taking in general. Don't let that stop you. Register for the test and take it as many times as you can until you pass it. Don't let fear stand in the way.

However, there are a few things you can do to soar past the fear and succeed at testing. That success depends on taking practice tests. Set up your practice tests to simulate the stress of test day. I want to recommend a few study methods that I had tremendous success with.

1. Read the NISPOM and paraphrase. Begin with paraphrasing the entire NISPOM into a few sentences. Then paraphrase each section independently. This will help you understand what each section (117.*) covers. In the earlier example, you might look at 117.2 and paraphrase the role each player has in the NISPOM application.

2. Enroll in DCSA's CDSE and take all the courses you can. Even if you know all of the material. Even if you don't have time, make the time to take all the course exams. Here's a helpful hint, download the PDF version of the course transcripts prior to taking the course exam. Then start the exam and practice searching for the answers. Even if you know the answers, search until you can find them.

3. Go through each question in this book and use an electronic version of 32 CFR Part 117 NISPOM to search for answers. A searchable 32 CFR Part 117 is available at ***https://www.redbikepublishing.com/ispcert/***

Even if you know the answer, do the search. This will give you practice and help increase your test taking confidence. Go through this book as many times as you can until you are confident that you can actually find the answers. Believe me, it will be a skill you will always need.

4. Set a timer. Use the questions in this book and searchable NISPOM, but set the timer for 120 minutes. Then set it for 90 minutes. Then try 60. The added pressure of a time line and even a condensed time line will make you more resilient on test day.

Are you ready? Then turn the page and begin practicing. Good luck!

PRACTICE TESTS

1. Use paperback copy or download online version of NISPOM to search for answers. Searchable 32 CFR Part 117 available at ***https://www.redbikepublishing.com/ispcert/***

2. Select the best answer for each choice.
3. Once complete, check your answers against the answer keys in the back of this book.

For practice purposes, download the electronic version of the NISPOM and use it to help search the answers to the provided test questions. Use a timer to count down 120 minutes for each practice exam.

This study guide is designed to be used in conjunction with both the electronic or hardcopy version of the NISPOM. By opening this manual, the hardcopy NISPOM or downloading the current electronic NISPOM, you can get tremendous practice. Just use the search function of the Adobe Acrobat NISPOM.

Warning: Not all questions will have searchable answers. It is important to understand the spirit of the question and know which part of the NISPOM contains the answer.

TEST 1

1. _____ Security Agreements are negotiated with various foreign governments.
a. Multi-force
b. Bi-lateral
c. Uni-lateral
d. Multi-lateral
e. Bi-layered

2. The _____ retains authority over access to intelligence methods and sources.
a. DNI
b. FBI
c. DCSA
d. CIA
e. SECDEF

3. The NISPOM also applies to classified information not released under a license, _____, grant, or certificate.
a. TAA
b. Contract
c. License
d. Scope
e. Registration

4. Which of the following are part of "DoD Components"?
a. Combatant Commands
b. Department of Justice
c. FBI
d. CIA
e. All of the above

5. Who is responsible to advise in the development of the Contract Security Classification Specification?
a. GCA
b. CSA
c. Contractor
d. DCSA
e. GCO

6. Contractors should train all _____ including outside of the U.S. of obligation to protect classified information.
a. Cleared employees
b. Company employees
c. Visitors
d. Temporary employees
e. All of the above

7. Which of the following characteristics is not used to describe a contractor?
a. Grantee
b. Certificate holder
c. Employee
d. Licensee
e. None of the above

8. Contractors shall submit reports to the:
a. FSO and DIA
b. FBI and CSA
c. CSO and DIA
d. FBI and CIA
e. CIA and DIA

9. Disclosure of U.S. Information to Foreign Governments is guided by the:
a. CSA
b. GCA
c. COR
d. ITAR
e. Exports Agreements

10. To which security clearance level is required for access to NATO RESTRICTED information?
a. TOP SECRET
b. SECRET
c. CONFIDENTIAL
d. RESTRICTED
e. None of the above

11. Which of the following are eligibility requirements a company must meet before it can be processed for an FCL?
a. The company must be an organization of at least twenty-five people
b. The company must have a desire for classified access
c. The company must have a reputation for integrity
d. The company must make its bottom line for three consecutive quarters
e. The company is the only entity that can perform the work

12. When can a contractor provide classified access to another contractor?
a. Furtherance of contract
b. Furtherance of business development
c. When directed by FSO
d. When directed by CSA
e. Just as long as other contractor is cleared

13. Unless restricted by the GCA, SECRET material may be reproduced as follows EXCEPT:
a. In performance of a prime contract
b. In performance of subcontract in furtherance of prime contract
c. Upon closure of contract

d. In preparation of patent applications
e. In preparation of bid to a Federal Agency

14. International visit requests include the following examples EXCEPT:
a. One-time
b. Recurring
c. Initial
d. Long-term
e. Emergency

15. Which are contractor inspection requirements required to reduce risk to classified information?
a. Perform inspections where unclassified work is performed
b. Perform inspections where classified work is performed
c. Post notices of inspections where possibility of access is remote
d. a and c
e. All of the above

16. Violations of export control regulations subjecting classified information to possible compromise by foreign nationals shall be reported to the:
a. GCA
b. Contractor
c. CSA
d. State Department
e. DGR

17. When sending a report for changes in cleared KMPs, what information must be included:
a. Level of clearance and when cleared, date and place of birth, social security numbers, citizenship, status of exclusion from access
b. Special accesses, citizenship, date of employment, date of birth and current address, date of facility clearance
c. Date of employment, clearance level and date, citizenship, social security number, status of exclusion from access
d. Special accesses, date and place of birth, social security number, date of employment, status of exclusion from access
e. Special access, level of clearance, citizenship

18. Which entities must be cleared to the same access level as the FCL?
a. Senior management official, FSO, KMP
b. FSO, KMP, ITPSO
c. FSO, senior management official, ITPSO
d. FSO, KMPs, all security personnel
e. All of the above

19. A contractor's information security system should use a _____ based approach to protect against unauthorized disclosure of classified information.
a. Confidentiality
b. Risk
c. Threat
d. Vulnerability
e. Availability

20. The ISs protection should be documented in the:
a. System Security Plan
b. Standard Operating Procedure
c. Insider Threat Plan
d. Program Protection Plan
e. All of the above

21. Reports submitted to the CSA include:
a. Sabotage
b. Espionage
c. Adverse Information
d. Acts of terrorism
e. None of the above

22. Risk Management Framework includes which of the following steps:
a. Categorized information processed on an IS
b. Assess and determine extent of security control implementation
c. Inventory IS components
d. a and b
e. All of the above

23. _____ have been used widely as set of best practices for authorizing and assessing information systems.
a. DoD 5220.22-M
b. DoDI 5200.44
c. NIST Risk Management Framework
d. CNSS I 1253
e. CNSS D 504

24. What are the appropriate steps to take in DISS when a cleared employee no longer needs a clearance but will remain with the company?
a. Admin Debrief
b. Debrief from access, separate from DISS
c. Separate from DISS, out process
d. Out process only
e. Separate from DISS only

25. What level of classified information should be maintained under an information management system?
a. CONFIDENTIAL
b. SECRET

c. TOP SECRET
d. b and c
e. All of the above

26. You must include information about all of the following EXCEPT on the SF86:
a. Parents
b. Cousins
c. Brothers
d. Sisters
e. Spouses

27. When must fingerprints be submitted?
a. For initial investigations and Periodic Review
b. For initial investigations only
c. For PR's only
d. At the completion of investigation
e. Never

28. Which E.O. provides guidance for safeguarding USG classified information?
a. E.O. 12353
b. E.O. 12829
c. E.O. 11257
d. E.O. 13691
e. E.O. 12563

29. Consultants can be cleared, however their performance on classified work is limited to:
a. The contractor facility unless in execution of authorized visits
b. Consultant home office with approved FCL
c. Consultant home office with contractor escort
d. Discretion of DD Form 254
e. All of the above

30. Some of the methods to mitigate or negate risks of foreign ownership or control include:
a. Board Resolution
b. Security Control Agreement
c. Special Security Agreement
d. a and c
e. All of the above

31. Required training under the Initial Security Briefing will include which of the following:
a. Threat awareness
b. Reporting obligations
c. Cleared Facility Orientation
d. a and b
e. All of the above

32. All contractor requests for interpretations of the NISPOM shall be forwarded through the _____ to the _____.

a. FBI, CSA
b. DCSA, CSA
c. DCSA, FBI
d. CSO only
e. CSA only

33. FSO qualifications include being a _____ and _____.

a. U.S. Citizen, cleared as part of FCL
b. U.S. Citizen, exempt from clearance
c. U.S. Citizen, certified as ISP
d. U.S. Citizen, attended college
e. U.S. Citizen, cleared to SCI

34. When a contractor challenges a classification, if no written answer is provided within 60 days, the contractor should request help from the _____.

a. CSA
b. GSA
c. GCA
d. FBI
e. FSO

35. Which organization acts as CSA for the DoD?

a. Secretary of Energy
b. Under Secretary of Defense for Intelligence & Security
c. Director DCSA
d. Director of National Intelligence
e. Director of DOJ

36. All attendees of meetings shall possess _____and _____.

a. Clearance, need to know
b. Clearance, ID card
c. Authorized tablet, pen
d. VAL, authorization
e. Clearance, authorization

37. Which of the following actions are required before the prime contractor may release or disclose classified information to a subcontractor?

a. Determine clearance status
b. Determine size of company
c. Determine capability to perform work on time
d. Determine type of business
e. Determine location of work performed

38. Where initial response teams consist of uncleared employees, which of the following response times apply?

a. 72 hours
b. 48 hours
c. A reasonable amount of time
d. 30 days
e. 45 days

39. A record of TOP SECRET material must be made when material is:

a. Completed as a finished document
b. Retained for more than 180 days of creation
c. Transmitted outside of the facility
d. None of the above
e. All of the above

40. SECRET material shall be stored in which of the following scenarios:

a. GSA approved security container
b. Approved vault
c. Closed areas
d. a and b (CFR 2001.43)
e. All of the above

41. Concerning a government contractor monitoring station with a response team cleared at the SECRET level, how many guards are required to respond to an alarm?

a. At least two when at least one guard is cleared
b. The amount sufficient to immediately investigate each alarm
c. At least five when at least one guard is cleared
d. At least four when at least one guard is cleared
e. At least three when at least one guard is cleared

42. Who determines need to know at classified meetings?

a. GCA
b. Contract monitor
c. Individual disclosing information
d. Visiting individuals
e. FSA

43. The structural integrity in closed areas should be ensured with:

a. Annual inspections
b. Monthly inspections
c. Contractor developed procedures
d. Inspections every three months
e. Whenever directed by CSA

44. Which E.O. provides guidance for safeguarding USG classified information?
a. E.O. 12353
b. E.O. 12829
c. E.O. 11257
d. E.O. 13691
e. E.O. 12563

45. How many days from the date access to cryptographic information is not needed must an employee be debriefed?
a. 30 days
b. 90 days
c. 180 days
d. Two years
e. One year

46. TOP SECRET information can be transmitted by which of the following methods within the U.S. and its territories:
a. Defense Courier Service, if authorized by GCA
b. A courier cleared at the SECRET level
c. By electrical means over FSO approved secured communication devices
d. By government vehicle
e. By U.S. Postal Service Registered Mail

47. SECRET information can be transmitted by which of the following means:
a. Registered mail
b. Cleared commercial carrier
c. As authorized by the GCA
d. Commercial company approved by CSA
e. All of the above

48. Couriers shall ensure all EXCEPT:
a. Information remains under constant protection
b. Information remains under continuous protection
c. They possess authorization to store classified in hotel safe
d. Locked briefcase may serve as outer layer
e. None of the above

50. The foreign government designation of RESTRICTED should be given what level of protection in the U. S. where bilateral security agreements exist:
a. SECRET
b. TOP SECRET
c. CONFIDENTIAL
d. UNCLASSIFIED
e. FOUO

51. May the CSA approve multiple stops while a contract employee hand-carries classified between countries?
a. Yes, if approved secure contractor storage is available
b. Never, only non-stop flights are authorized
c. Yes, if approved secure government storage is available
d. Yes, as long as classified never leaves courier sight
e. None of the above

52. Which of the following are types of international visit request?
a. Initial
b. Follow-up
c. Amendment
d. Special
e. Annual

53. If retention of classified documents under an expired contract is desired for longer than the two year period, who is the approval authority?
a. GCA
b. CSA
c. FSO
d. FBI
e. CSO

54. What is the primary disposition of classified documents where retention has not been authorized?
a. Disseminate to winning bid contractor
b. Destroy unless declassified
c. Maintain on site
d. a and c
e. None of the above

55. Destruction records are required for:
a. TOP SECRET
b. SECRET
c. CONFIDENTIAL
d. a and b
e. All of the above

56. Construction in closed areas should be built of material that:
a. Prevents opening by magnetic pulse
b. Prevents opening by shotgun blast
c. Provides evidence of unauthorized access
d. Protects from bomb blasts
e. a and c

57. Vents with openings greater than 96 inches and over _____inches at smallest measurement shall be protected.

a. 2
b. 6
c. 9
d. 10
e. 18

58. How many employees must be working at a SECRET cleared central station?

a. Two
b. Five
c. Enough to sufficiently monitor each cleared contractors alarmed area
d. One as long as there is a quick reaction team
e. None of the above

59. Which of the following resources are authorized to investigate alarms at a cleared contractor facility?

a. Local police force
b. FBI
c. Fire department
d. Subcontracted guards
e. Military police

60. The requirement for on time response for alarms is:

a. 75%
b. 85%
c. 90%
d. 65%
e. 80%

61. Persons attending classified meetings must have the proper _____:

a. Clearance and need to know
b. Clearance and authority
c. Authority and need to know
d. Access and reporting authority
e. Accountability and authenticity

62. Repairs of approved containers include which of the following procedures:

a. Damaged or altered parts are replaced with manufacturer's replacement
b. Damaged or altered parts replaced with identical cannibalized parts
c. Damaged or altered parts are repaired with other than approved methods if storing SECRET material under supplemental controls until October 1, 2012
d. According to FED STD 809
e. All of the above

63. Which statement is true of government officials visiting a contractor facility?

a. They must relinquish control of their work product
b. Classified work product must be handled according to GCA regulations

c. Government employees are not required to relinquish work product unless it is classified
d. Presents appropriate credentials
e. None of the above

64. An information system's security efforts should include a baseline set of _______, _______, and technical controls.
a. Management, Operational
b. Visual, Audible
c. Standardized, Authentic
d. Risk Based, Authentic
e. Availability, Integrity

65. Which of the following is true about information system passwords
a. Protected in the same manner as information on the system
b. Protected at the same level as the information on the system
c. Changed in frequency to meet the level of risk assessed by CSA
d. a and c
e. All of the above

66. Who approves security changes to an IS?
a. ISSM
b. GCA
c. FSO
d. ISSO
e. CSA

67. Under SEAD and CSA guidance, what should contractors report?
a. Provide general information about protection of classified information
b. Provide reports to CSA, FBI and ISOO as required
c. Reports should be from the cleared employee to the CSA
d. When reports are classified, the Privacy Act does not apply to reports
e. All of the above

68. Storing information in a _____ may be necessary when other normal means are unsuitable or impractical:
a. Supplemental protection
b. Closed area
c. Open area
d. Restricted area
e. None of the above

69. Reference numbers on US originated NATO documents must be on _____ of a document:
a. Each page of the document
b. The front and back covers
c. The first page
d. The title and first pages
e. The appendix page

70. Recommendations for the declassification of NATO classified information should be forwarded to:
a. Originating activity
b. CSA
c. CISSP
d. CUSR
e. FSCC

71. Verification of a meeting, the attendee's identity is verified by official photographic identification such as:
a. Passport
b. Contractor ID
c. Military ID
d. CAC card
e. All of the above

72. If a prospective subcontractor does not have the appropriate FCL, or safeguarding capability, the _____ shall request the CSA of the _____ to initiate the necessary action.
a. Subcontractor, prime contractor
b. Prime contractor, GCA
c. Prime contractor, subcontractor
d. GCA, prime contractor
e. GCA, subcontractor

73. A contractor is any _____ entity that has been granted an FCL by the CSA
a. Educational
b. Industrial
c. Commercial
d. Other
e. All of the above

74. If a cleared facility hosts a government sponsored classified meeting, which of the following must be approved by the government?
a. Menu
b. Seating order
c. Announcements
d. Slide show background
e. Dress code

75. When taking action to downgrade classified information, the contractor must seek guidance from:
a. GSA
b. CSA
c. GCA
d. FBI
e. CSO

76. Which of the following apply to end of day security checks?
a. Perform checks at the close of each working day

b. Perform checks at end of last shift in which classified material was removed for use
c. Not necessary during continuing 24 hour operations
d. a and c
e. All of the above

77. An original Contract Security Classification Specification shall be included with each:
a. RFQ
b. RFP
c. IFB
d. Other solicitation
e. All of the above

78. If an ISSO is designated to conduct self-inspections, they should provide results to the:
a. GCA
b. FSO
c. CSA
d. ISSM
e. GSA

79. An employee may be processed for a PCL when the ______ determines access is essential.
a. Contractor
b. CSO
c. GCA
d. CSA
e. ISSM

80. Which E.O. provides information on marking classified email?
a. E.O. 12353
b. E.O. 13526
c. E.O. 11257
d. E.O. 13691
e. E.O. 12563

81. Concerning meetings, the _____ shall create security requirements and get the _____ approval.
a. Contractor, FSO
b. Contractor, CSA
c. FSO, CSA
d. CSA, authorizing agency
e. Contractor, authorizing agency

82. Which is a responsibility of the Secretary of Energy?
a. Authority for procedures for information classified under AEA
b. Authority over access to information classified under AEA
c. Authority over portions pertaining to information classified as RD
d. Authority over portions pertaining to information classified as FRD
e. All of the above

83. Who has responsibility for assessing information systems?
a. CSA and Contractor
b. FSO and ISSM
c. ISSM and ISSO
d. ISSO and GCA
e. CSA and GCA

84. Which change conditions are contractors required to report that may impact security clearance status?
a. Change of control of contractor
b. Change in contractor ownership
c. Significant stock transfers
d. a and c
e. All of the above

85. Which of the following apply to conducting inspections?
a. All persons entering or exiting are subject to search
b. Limit searches to buildings where classified work is performed
c. Perform inspections on a random basis
d. Not necessary where possible access to classified material is remote
e. All of the above (NISPOM 117.15)

86. Contractors shall conduct the self-inspections at iterations consistent with:
a. Risk management principles
b. DCSA inspection dates
c. FSO determination
d. Previous results
e. All of the above

87. Under the certification and accreditation, the old term certification now crosswalks to the RMF term _____.
a. Authorization
b. System Security plan
c. Security Controls
d. Assessment
e. Impact

88. What should contractors ensure their derivative classifiers accomplish?
a. Be an original classifier
b. Complete derivative classifier training
c. Complete a waiver if derivative classifier training is not available
d. Complete FSO certification training
e. a and c

89. Which of the following are appropriate portion markings found on classified documents?
a. SECRET, TOP SECRET, CONFIDENTIAL
b. S, TS, C

c. UNCLASSIFIED, TS, CONFIDENTIAL
d. FSO, TS, C, U
e. All of the above

90. The _____ has authority pertaining to access to intelligence methods and sources.
a. NSA
b. DoD
c. DNI
d. DOA
e. GCA

91. Contractors shall report all unauthorized disclosure concerning RD and FRD to the:
a. DOE
b. NRC
c. CSA
d. GCA
e. FSO

92. The minimum investigation requirements for TOP SECRET Q is:
a. Investigative tier appropriate for moderate risk positions
b. investigative tier appropriate for non-critical sensitive positions
c. investigative tier appropriate for high risk positions
d. a and b
e. None of the above

93. The minimum investigation requirements for CONFIDENTIAL PCL is:
a. Investigative tier appropriate for moderate risk positions
b. Investigative tier appropriate for high risk positions
c. Investigative tier appropriate for high critical sensitive positions
d. Investigative tier appropriate for special sensitive positions
e. Investigative tier appropriate for critical sensitive positions

94. Challenges to improperly classified RD/FRD documents should be addressed through the:
a. GCA
b. CSA
c. DOE
d. DoD
e. NRC

95. Contractors shall not disclose CNWDI to subcontractors without approval of the:
a. CSA
b. GCA
c. DOE
d. NRC
e. FSO

96. For government sponsored classified meetings at contractor facilities, who is responsible for assuming security jurisdiction?
a. The cleared contractor
b. The subcontracted security force
c. Authorizing government agency
d. Proprietary guard force
e. CSA

97. The _____ shall develop the security measures and obtain the _____ approval.
a. Contractor, FSO
b. Contractor, CSA
c. FSO, CSA
d. CSA, authorizing agency
e. Contractor, authorizing agency

98. NATO visit records must be kept for:
a. Two years
b. Three years
c. One year
d. 180 days
e. Four years

99. The NISP was established by:
a. Executive Order 12829
b. Executive Order 12333
c. Executive Order 13355
d. Executive Order 12356
e. Executive Order 12345

100. Which of the following are NOT listed as Proscribed Information?
a. TOP SECRET
b. SECRET
c. COMSEC
d. RD
e. SAP

101. TOP SECRET material shall be stored in a(n):
a. GSA approved security container
b. Approved vault
c. Approved closed area with supplemental controls
d. a and c
e. All of the above

102. Before COMSEC can be released to a contractor, the _____ must verify with the _____ that appropriate procedures are in place.
a. CSA, FSO
b. GCA, FSO

c. NSA, FSO
d. GCA, CSA
e. DIA, NSA

103. The _____ establishes the COMSEC account and notifies the CSA.
a. COR
b. GCA
c. FSO
d. NSA
e. DIA

104. Requirements for access to CRYPTO include the following EXCEPT:
a. U.S. citizenship
b. Valid need-to-know
c. CI scope polygraph
d. Appropriately cleared with a final security clearance
e. Appropriately briefed

105. The NISPOM prescribes the _____, _____, and other _____ to prevent unauthorized disclosure of classified information.
a. Standards, values, restrictions
b. Requirements, restrictions, safeguards
c. Date, time, measures
d. Content, procedures, standards
e. Date, procedures, safeguards

106. The _____ has been designated Executive Agent for the NISP by the President.
a. National Security Council
b. Secretary of State
c. Director of National Intelligence
d. Director of the CIA
e. Secretary of Defense

107. _____ Security Agreements are negotiated with various foreign governments.
a. Multi-force
b. Bi-lateral
c. Uni-lateral
d. Multi-lateral
e. Bi-layered

108. Foreign nationals can participate in classified gatherings if authorized by the head of the _____ authorizing the meeting.
a. U.S. Government Agency
b. FSO
c. CSO
d. Contractor
e. None of the above

109. The failure of a foreign entity to provide classification guidance should be reported to the:
a. Contracts manager
b. GCA
c. CSA
d. FSO
e. COR

110. Reproduction of foreign TOP SECRET information requires approval of the:
a. GCA
b. Originating Government
c. CSA
d. State Department
e. None of the above

TEST 2

1. The NISP was established by:
a. Executive Order 12829
b. Executive Order 12333
c. Executive Order 13355
d. Executive Order 12356
e. Executive Order 12345

2. An employee with a privileged user account can perform which of the following functions?
a. System Control
b. System Monitoring
c. Data Transfer
d. Functions general users are not authorized to perform
e. All of the above

3. General and privileged users should receive which of the following training?
a. Threat awareness training
b. Insider threat training
c. Risks associated with user activities
d. NISP based responsibilities
e. All of the above

4. Contractors performing work on federal installations shall safeguard classified information according to procedures of:
a. NISPOM
b. Block 13 of DD Form 254
c. Host Installation or Agency
d. CSA
e. CSO

5. Contractors shall establish procedures for _____notification after death or incapacitation.
a. CSA
b. GCA
c. Next of kin
d. FSO
e. FBI

6. Reports submitted to the _____ involve espionage, terrorism and sabotage.
a. CIA
b. FSO
c. CSA
d. ISSM
e. FBI

7. Consultants can be cleared, however their performance on classified work is limited to:
a. The contractor facility unless in execution of authorized visits
b. Consultant home office with approved FCL
c. Consultant home office with contractor escort
d. Discretion of DD Form 254
e. All of the above

8. Contractors are permitted to implement downgrading or declassification upon guidance or notification from?
a. CSA
b. CSO
c. GSA
d. GCA
e. None of the above

9. International visit requests include the following examples EXCEPT:
a. One-time
b. Recurring
c. Initial
d. Long-term
e. Emergency

10. Selections for types of visit on the visit request form include:
a. Initial
b. Follow-up
c. Amendment
d. Special
e. Annual

11. Which positions must be cleared to the same access level of the FCL?
a. Senior management official and Insider Threat Program Senior Official
b. FSO and KMP's
c. FSO and senior management official
d. a and c
e. b and c

12. An authorization is required _____ a contractor makes an export proposal to a foreign interest that involves release of U.S. classified information.
a. When
b. Before
c. After
d. Unless
e. None of the above

13. The _____ shall identify the recipient government's DGR and appoint a U.S. DGR.
a. COR
b. CSA
c. FSO
d. GCA
e. State Department

14. Which of the following are appropriate portion markings found on classified documents?
a. SECRET, TOP SECRET, CONFIDENTIAL
b. S, TS, C
c. UNCLASSIFIED, TS, CONFIDENTIAL
d. FSO, TS, C, U
e. All of the above

15. The moderate risk, non-critical sensitive tier is required for access to classified information up to which levels?
a. CONFIDENTIAL, L, and SECRET PCLs
b. TOPSECRET, Q, and SCI access
c. TOP SECRET
d. a and c
e. SECRET only

16. The Secretary of Energy or the Chairman of the Nuclear Regulatory Commission are responsible for prescribing procedure for:
a. Portions of this rule that pertain to information under DNI programs
b. Portions of this rule that pertain to information under DOE programs
c. Portions of this rule that pertain to information under NRC programs
d. Portions of this rule that pertain to information under SAP programs
e. None of the above

17. The _____ will address complaints and suggestions with respect to the administration of the NISP.
a. Secretary of Defense
b. Director of FBI
c. Defense Security Services
d. Director of ISOO
e. Cognizant Security Agency

18. Which of the following is not a risk designation for security clearances?
a. Positions designated as moderate risk
b. Positions designated as medium risk
c. Positions designated as high risk
d. Positions designated as low risk
e. None of the above

19. For a Tier 3 investigation you must provide work experience for the past _____ years.
a. Ten
b. Twenty
c. Seven
d. Five
e. Three

20. How long does a security clearance remain in effect?
a. Forever
b. five years for TS
c. ten years for S
d. As long as employed and expected to require access to classified information
e. b and c

21. Who conducts security clearance investigations for the DoD?
a. Each cleared contractor is required to pay for investigations
b. FBI
c. DCSA
d. OPM
e. CAF

22. How many days must the employee begin work after a PCL is granted according to the commitment for employment?
a. 60 days
b. 45 days
c. 180 days
d. 90 days
e. 56 days

23. Which of the following are part of "DoD Components"?
a. DOE
b. DOJ
c. FBI
d. CIA
e. Military Departments

24. From whom would a contractor receive a facility clearance assurance for a foreign entity?
a. CSA
b. Cleared contractor
c. GCA
d. Sponsoring government's security authority
e. Department of State

25. Derivative Classification includes:
a. Incorporated classified information
b. Restated classified information
c. Generate classified information in a new form

d. All of the above
e. b and c

26. To whom does a contractor initially submit classification challenges?
a. GCA
b. CSA
c. FSO
d. FBI
e. GSA

27. Required security training and briefing titles include:
a. Initial security briefings, refresher, annual briefings
b. Initial security briefings, annual, debriefings
c. Initial security briefings, Insider threat training, CUI training
d. Annual, refresher, initial security briefings
e. Initial security briefings, annual, refresher

28. Contractors shall conduct formal self inspections at intervals consistent with:
a. At least annually and according to risk management principles
b. DCSA inspection dates
c. FSO determination
d. Previous results
e. All of the above

29. All classified information and material should be marked to clearly convey:
a. Level of classification
b. Portions that reveal classified
c. Portions that contain classified
d. Period of time protection is required
e. All of the above

30. NATO has the following levels of security classification EXCEPT:
a. COSMIC TOP SECRET
b. NATO SECRET
c. NATO CONFIDENTIAL
d. NATO RESTRICTED
e. NATO TOP SECRET

31. In situations of classified information inadvertently released as UNCLASSIFIED, the contractor's notice shall be classified _____ unless it contains information for higher classification.
a. UNCLASSIFIED
b. FOR OFFICIAL USE ONLY
c. SECRET
d. TOP SECRET
e. CONFIDENTIAL

32. Which of the following contract information requires GCA approval before release to the public?
a. Release of unclassified information on a classified contract
b. The fact that a contract has been received
c. The method of contract
d. The fact that a contract is negotiated
e. Whether or not contract requires hiring or terminating of employees

33. Which are contractor inspection requirements required to reduce risk to classified information?
a. Perform inspections where unclassified work is performed
b. Perform inspections where classified work is performed
c. Post notices of inspections where possibility of access is remote
d. a and c
e. All of the above

34. Contractors shall maintain a record of destruction of SECRET material for _____ years.
a. Two years
b. One year
c. Five years
d. Thirty days
e. None of the above

35. Controlling access to classified material in an open area during working hours is an example of:
a. Supplemental protection
b. Establishing a closed area
c. Establishing an open area
d. Establishing a restricted area
e. None of the above

36. For NATO accountability records, titles should not contain:
a. Reference number
b. Short title
c. Classification level
d. Classified information
e. All of the above

37. CONFIDENTIAL is approved for transmission by which of the following means?
a. U.S. Postal Service Priority Mail
b. U.S. Postal Service First Class Mail
c. Any commercial overnight delivery company
d. U.S. Postal Service Certified Mail
e. All of the above

38. Authorization in writing by the _____ is required for transmission of TOP SECRET outside of a facility while the electrical transmission means over _______ approved secured communications security circuits.
a. CSA, GSA
b. CSA, FSO

c. FSO, DOT
d. CSA, DOT
e. GCA, CSA

39. What should be provided in an escort's written instructions prior to shipping classified information?
a. Receipt procedures
b. Means of transportation
c. Emergency communication procedures
d. Route to be used
e. All of the above

40. When is a company under FOCI eligible for a security clearance?
a. When FSO has submitted final report
b. Once security measures to mitigate or negate FOCI are established
c. When FSO completes OPSEC report
d. Upon completion of foreign interest visit
e. Upon completion of initial report

41. If required, the FSO Program Management Course should be complete within _____ of appointment to the position of FSO.
a. 30 days
b. 90 days
c. Three months
d. Six months
e. One year

42. Which government agency has jurisdiction over RD?
a. NSA
b. FRD
c. DNI
d. CSA
e. DOE

43. How often must contractors review security programs?
a. On a recurring basis
b. Monthly
c. Within 180 days of accountability
d. Before contract end
e. Annually during inventory

44. Receipts must be provided for which level of classified material?
a. SECRET
b. CONFIDENTIAL
c. UNCLASSIFIED
d. a and b
e. All of the above

45. Working papers shall be marked the same as finished documents and at the same classification level. Which answer is correct concerning retention?

a. Transmitted within the facility
b. Retained for more than 30 days from creation for TOP SECRET
c. Retained for more than 180 days from creation for SECRET
d. Retained for more than 120 days from creation for SECRET
e. Retained for more than 120 days from creation for CONFIDENTIAL

46. Classified material may be destroyed by which of the following methods?

a. Mutilation
b. Chemical decomposition
c. Pulverization
d. Melting
e. All of the above

47. Which E.O. provides information on marking classified email?

a. E.O. 12353
b. E.O. 13526
c. E.O. 11257
d. E.O. 13691
e. E.O. 12563

48. Which of the following apply to conducting inspections?

a. All persons entering or exiting are subject to search
b. Limit searches to buildings where classified work is performed
c. Perform inspections on a random basis
d. Not necessary where possible access to classified material is remote
e. All of the above

49. The contractor shall forward the names of employees who shall serve as COMSEC and alternate COMSEC account managers to the _____.

a. GCA
b. FSO
c. CSA
d. NSA
e. COR

50. Contractors must obtain written approval from the _____ before subcontracting COMSEC work.

a. COR
b. NSA
c. DIA
d. CSA
e. GCA

51. Government representatives serving in an official capacity may visit a contractor facility in which of the following circumstances?
a. Official capacity as inspectors
b. When presenting appropriate identification
c. Official capacity as auditors
d. Official capacity as investigators
e. All of the above

52. ______ issues protective measures and guidance on protection of ISs.
a. GCA
b. ISSO
c. FSO
d. CSA
e. NISPOM

53. Where initial response teams consist of uncleared employees, which of the following response times apply?
a. 72 hours
b. 48 hours
c. A reasonable amount of time
d. 30 days
e. 45 days

54. Which of the following is true about information system passwords
a. Protected in the same manner as information on the system
b. Protected at the same level as the information on the system
c. Changed in frequency to meet the level of risk assessed by CSA
d. a and c
e. All of the above

55. When sending a report for changes in cleared KMPs, which information must be included?
a. Level of clearance and when cleared, date and place of birth, social security numbers, citizenship, status of exclusion from access
b. Special accesses, citizenship, date of employment, date of birth and current address, date of facility clearance
c. Date of employment, clearance level and date, citizenship, social security number, status of exclusion from access
d. Special accesses, date and place of birth, social security number, date of employment, status of exclusion from access
e. Special access, level of clearance, citizenship

56. The system security program should be delegated by the:
a. FSO
b. ISSO
c. CSA
d. SSM
e. System user

57. Which of the following are types of international visit request?
a. Initial
b. Follow-up
c. Amendment
d. Special
e. Annual

58. If a cleared facility hosts a government sponsored classified meeting, which of the following must be approved by the government?
a. Menu
b. Seating order
c. Announcements
d. Slide show background
e. Dress code

59. Which organization approves use of IDS?
a. FSO
b. CSO
c. CSA
d. GCA
e. GSA

60. Response times for investigating alarms shall not exceed:
a. Thirty minutes
b. Fifteen minutes
c. Twenty minutes
d. One hour
e. What is reasonable to safeguard classified material

61. All attendees of classified meetings shall possess _____ and _____.
a. Clearance, need to know
b. Clearance, ID card
c. Authorized tablet, pen
d. VAL, authorization
e. Clearance, authorization

62. What is one of the required actions necessary before a prime contractor may release or disclose classified information to a subcontractor?
a. Determine clearance status
b. Determine size of company
c. Determine capability to perform work on time
d. Determine type of business
e. Determine location of work performed

63. Construction in closed areas should be built of material that:
a. Prevents opening by magnetic pulse
b. Prevents opening by shotgun blast
c. Provides evidence of unauthorized access
d. Protects from bomb blasts
e. a and c

64. Vents with openings greater than 96 inches and over _____inches at smallest measurement shall be protected.
a. 2
b. 6
c. 9
d. 10
e. 18

65. Contractors must obtain _____ approval before installing Intrusion Detection Systems.
a. CSS
b. CSA
c. GCA
d. GSA
e. DIA

66. Which of the following reflect the bilateral security agreement?
a. Requires each government to provide different degrees of protection
b. Provides restrictions for third party transfers
c. Allows for unlimited use of information and third party transfers
d. Doesn't meet requirements found in the Arms Export Control Act
e. None of the above

67. Open bin storage is not allowed for:
a. TOP SECRET
b. SECRET
c. CONFIDENTIAL
d. UNCLASSIFIED
e. a and b

68. What level of classified information should be maintained under an information management system?
a. CONFIDENTIAL
b. SECRET
c. TOP SECRET
d. b and c
e. All of the above

69. Which organization ensures FSOs receive briefings for special categories of information?
a. CSA
b. GCA
c. ISSM
d. FSO
e. GSA

70. Who is responsible for providing initial security briefings to the FSO?
a. DSSA
b. FSO
c. CSO
d. GCA
e. CSA

71. A contractor is any educational, industrial, commercial, other entity that has been granted an FCL by the:
a. GCA
b. DIA
c. CIA
d. GSA
e. CSA

72. The _____ chooses controls, the _____provides set of security controls, and _____ acknowledges risk.
a. Contractor, CSA, USG
b. ISSO, ISSM, CSA
c. ISSO, GCA, CSA
d. CSA, Contractor, GSA
e. ISSO, GSA, GCA

73. Need to know is generally based on:
a. Level of clearance
b. Block 13 of DD Form 254
c. Security Classification Guide
d. Contractual relationship
e. As determined by CSA

74. Which entities must be cleared to the same access level as the FCL?
a. Senior management official, FSO, KMP
b. FSO, KMP, ITPSO
c. FSO, senior management official, ITPSO
d. FSO, KMPs, all security personnel
e. All of the above

75. The duties of the ISSM include:
a. Have oversight of the development of the contractor's IS program
b. Serve as the Authorization to Operate Authority
c. Issue protective measure guidance

d. Designate security control profiles
e. Provide guidelines for operational and technical controls

76. Which of the following apply to end of day security checks?
a. Perform checks at the close of each working day
b. Perform checks at end of last shift in which classified material was removed for use
c. Not necessary during continuing 24 hour operations
d. a and c
e. All of the above

77. The NISPOM requires the frequency of classified visits be:
a. No more than one per week
b. Unlimited as long as FSO's keep a log
c. Unlimited due to Freedom of Information Act
d. Kept to a minimum
e. Determined by amount of classified contracts

78. Continuous evaluation uses _____ and ______ in the assessment of security clearance eligibility.
a. records checks, business rules
b. Certification, Accreditation
c. investigations, questionnaires
d. Analysis, Prioritization
e. Authorization, Accreditation

79. TOP SECRET information should be made a permanent record when:
a. A temporary product
b. Retained for 90 days or fewer
c. Transmitted outside of the facility
d. Retained for 120 days or fewer
e. None of the above

80. Which organization has the ability to authorize information systems used to process classified information?
a. CSA
b. GSA
c. ISSM
d. ISSO
e. GCA

81. Storing information in a _____ may be necessary when other normal means are unsuitable or impractical:
a. Supplemental protection
b. Closed area
c. Open area
d. Restricted area
e. None of the above

82. Which organization certifies that an information system incorporates a protection program that includes CSA required controls?
a. CSA
b. GSA
c. Contractor
d. None of the above
e. All of the above

83. The management of classified IS primarily concerns prevention of:
a. Loss of confidentiality
b. Loss of integrity
c. Loss of availability
d. Unauthorized disclosure of classified information
e. None of the above

84. If a contractor believes information to be classified when it was not originally identified as classified, the contractor should:
a. Hold the information as unclassified until determination is made
b. Return to the customer through same method as delivered
c. Protect as classified and return to proper agency
d. Mark as classified and store with similar classified items
e. Destroy the item

85. Which of the following should be included in an information system's security program?
a. Risk reducing policies and procedures
b. Adequate information security plans for classified data on IS
c. A methodology for implementing mitigations addressing IS policy gaps
d. Ability to evaluate IS security controls
e. Plans and procedures to assess, report, isolate, and contain data spills and compromises, to include sanitization and recovery methods

86. What should contractors ensure their derivative classifiers accomplish?
a. Be an original classifier
b. Complete derivative classifier training
c. Complete a waiver if derivative classifier training is not available
d. Complete FSO certification training
e. a and c

87. Which are processes of the RMF?
a. Prepare
b. Categorize
c. Select
d. a and b
e. All of the above

88. Which of the following can grant access to RD and FRD?
a. DOE
b. NRC
c. DoD
d. NASA
e. All of the above

89. Alternative Compensatory Control Measures include items identified as:
a. SECRET
b. CONFIDENTIAL
c. SAP
d. TOP SECRET
e. None of the above

90. Only contractors with ______ may classify or upgrade matter containing RD and FRD.
a. FRD Classifiers
b. RD derivative classification authority
c. NRC Classifiers
d. DOE Classifiers
e. DoD Classifiers

91. _____ is a DoD category of TOP SECRET Restricted Data or SECRET Restricted Data that reveals operation of components of a thermonuclear bomb.
a. CNWDI
b. FRD
c. RD
d. NATO
e. EWNDI

92. Water repellent papers shall be destroyed by:
a. Shredding
b. Burning
c. Disintegration
d. Pulping
e. a, b, or c

93. Working papers shall be marked the same as finished documents and at the same classification level. Which answer is correct concerning retention?
a. Transmitted within the facility
b. Retained for more than 30 days from creation for TOP SECRET
c. Retained for more than 180 days from creation for SECRET
d. Retained for more than 120 days from creation for SECRET
e. Retained for more than 120 days from creation for CONFIDENTIAL

94. Employees shall sign a certificate stating that they have been given a NATO security briefing. Certificates for NATO CONFIDENTIAL must be maintained for:
a. Three years
b. Two years
c. Five years
d. Seven years
e. Four years

95. Suspected loss or compromise of classified information must be reported to the:
a. FBI
b. GSA
c. CSA
d. ISSO
e. SGM

96. Which organization acts as CSA for the DoD?
a. Secretary of Energy
b. Under Secretary of Defense for Intelligence & Security
c. Director DCSA
d. Director of National Intelligence
e. Director of DOJ

97. Under SEAD and CSA guidance, what should contractors report?
a. Provide general information about protection of classified information
b. Provide reports to CSA, FBI and ISOO as required
c. Reports should be from the cleared employee to the CSA
d. When reports are classified, the Privacy Act does not apply to reports
e. All of the above

98. How many days from the date access to cryptographic information is not needed must an employee be debriefed?
a. 30 days
b. 90 days
c. 180 days
d. Two years
e. One year

99. For international transfers, if the courier doesn't arrive within _____ hours of anticipated delivery time, the receiving security officer must notify the dispatching security officer.
a. 36 hours
b. 10 hours
c. 24 hours
d. 8 hours
e. 4 hours

101. All of the following require destruction certificates EXCEPT:
a. NATO SECRET
b. NATO SECRET ATOMAL
c. COSMIC TOP SECRET
d. NATO CONFIDENTIAL
e. NATO CONFIDENTIAL ATOMAL

102. Which of the following characteristics is not used to describe a contractor?
a. Grantee
b. Certificate holder
c. Employee
d. None of the above
e. Licensee

103. Which E.O. provides information on marking classified email?
a. E.O. 12353
b. E.O. 13526
c. E.O. 11257
d. E.O. 13691
e. E.O. 12563

104. Which agency has classification authority and can authorize release of COMSEC information to a foreign person?
a. NSA
b. DIA
c. CIA
d. DoD
e. DOE

105. The FSO, COMSEC and alternate COMSEC account managers shall be briefed by the _____ or their designee.
a. Government representative
b. KMP
c. FSO
d. COR
e. Outgoing custodian

106. Initial reports submitted to the FBI must be followed up by:
a. Telephone reports and submitted to CSA in writing
b. Written reports and a copy submitted to CSA
c. Face to face reports and submitted to CSA in writing
d. a and b
e. All of the above

107. The structural integrity in closed areas should be ensured with:
a. Annual inspections
b. Monthly inspections
c. Contractor developed procedures
d. Inspections every three months
e. Whenever directed by CSA

108. The _____ provides the security classification guides.
a. FSO
b. CSA
c. GCA
d. DoD
e. Secretary of Defense

109. Which change conditions are contractors required to report that may impact security clearance status?
a. Change of control of contractor
b. Change in contractor ownership
c. Significant stock transfers
d. a and c
e. All of the above

110. Which is not a reportable event that impacts the status of PCLs and FCLs?
a. Contractors did not attend Prevention of Sexual Harassment Training
b. Employee is an insider threat
c. Security containers are often left unlocked and unattended
d. Classified laptop was stolen from a government vehicle
e. Classified notebook was stolen from a privately owned vehicle

TEST 3

1. The _____ or _____ may inspect and monitor contractor, licensee, grantee, and certificate holder programs and facilities.
a. Secretary of Defense, NRC
b. Secretary of Energy, Secretary of Defense
c. Secretary of Energy, FBI
d. Secretary of Defense, DCSA
e. Secretary of Energy, Chairman of NRC

2. The requirement for heads of agencies to enter into agreement with the Secretary of Defense as the Executive agent for the NISP is:
a. 32 CFR part 2004
b. Executive order 12958
c. NISPOM
d. Executive Order 12929
e. ITAR

3. The CSA shall forward the names of cleared and briefed employees who shall serve as FSO, COMSEC and alternate COMSEC custodians to the:
a. COR, GCA
b. NSA
c. DoD
d. DIA
e. DOE

4. "The transfer of technical data, articles, and _____ to foreign persons…constitutes an export".
a. Services
b. Books
c. Tools
d. Weapons
e. Aircraft

5. Which E.O. provides guidance for safeguarding USG classified information?
a. E.O. 12353
b. E.O. 12829
c. E.O. 11257
d. E.O. 13691
e. E.O. 12563

6. Requests for NISPOM interpretation by contractors on U.S. Government installations should be sent to the _____ via the Commander.
a. CSO
b. President
c. GCA
d. Translator
e. CSA

7. SPP's shall be certified in writing by the _____ to the ____ that the plan is implemented.
a. CSA, CSO
b. FBI, FSO
c. FSO, CSA
d. CSA, SECDEF
e. CSA, FBI

8. Which is a responsibility of the Secretary of Energy?
a. Authority for procedures for information classified under AEA
b. Authority over access to information classified under AEA
c. Authority over portions pertaining to information classified as RD
d. Authority over portions pertaining to information classified as FRD
e. All of the above

9. _____ shall provide security training to cleared employees and advise them of obligations to protect classified information.
a. CSA
b. DSSA
c. CSO
d. FSO
e. Contractors

10. Contractors shall submit corrective actions taken against an employee to the CSA when it is determined that the employee is responsible for a security violation and _____ is evident:
a. The violation involved a deliberate disregard of security requirements
b. The violation was just a one-time incident without violation of procedure
c. The violation was not deliberate and did not involve a pattern of negligence
d. The violator was not remorseful
e. The violation happened in spite of the excellent care in the handling of classified material

11. How long must a contractor maintain original CSA designated forms?
a. Duration of the contract and DD Form 254
b. Two years
c. For the FCL duration
d. Five years
e. When contractor has significant change in status

12. Concerning IS privileges, all users shall:
a. Have access to IS control
b. Have access to IS monitoring
c. Act as Designated Accreditation/Approving Authority
d. Accredit information systems used to process classified information
e. Be accountable for actions on an IS

13. International visit requests include the following examples EXCEPT:
a. One-time
b. Recurring

c. Initial
d. Long-term
e. Emergency

14. Contractors shall deny cleared employee access to classified information when notified of:
a. Removal from JPAS, denial of clearance, revocation of clearance
b. Termination of employment, suspension or denial of clearance
c. Denial, revocation or suspension of clearance
d. Removal from JPAS, adverse information, disclosure of classified information
e. Excessive drinking, debt, or unexplained affluence

15. The Tier 5 Investigation is required for:
a. SECRET, L, and CONFIDENTIAL PCLs
b. TOP SECRET, Q, and SCI access
c. TOP SECRET only
d. SECRET only
e. All of the above

16. For an active DISS account status one must log in every _____ days.
a. 60
b. 90
c. 30
d. 45
e. 180

17. Which fields are required for looking up a person in DISS?
a. Last name
b. First and last name
c. Social Security Number and last name
d. First, middle and last name and Social Security Number
e. Social Security Number

18. For a Tier 5 investigation, you must provide work experience for the past _____ years.
a. 10
b. 20
c. Seven
d. Five
e. Three

19. The FSO or designee shall review the SF 86 to determine:
a. Adequacy and accuracy
b. Completeness and accuracy
c. Adequacy and completeness
d. Accuracy and timeliness
e. Completeness and timeliness

20. What level of classified information should be maintained under an information management system?
a. CONFIDENTIAL
b. SECRET
c. TOP SECRET
d. b and c
e. All of the above

21. Where initial response teams consist of uncleared employees, which of the following response times apply?
a. 72 hours
b. 48 hours
c. A reasonable amount of time
d. 30 days
e. 45 days

22. In which situations are contractors permitted to grant clearances?
a. If work begins within 30 days of granting FCL or PCL
b. Under supervision of CSA
c. Never
d. If necessary for performance on contract
e. When directed by CSA

23. The SF 312 is an agreement between _____ and _____.
a. FSO, individual
b. FSO, CSA
c. United States, FSO
d. United states, cleared individual
e. CSA, individual

24. Methods of approved refresher training include:
a. Briefings
b. Instructional materials
c. Videos
d. All of the above
e. a and c

25. Export control regulation violations subjecting classified information to be compromised by foreign nationals shall be reported to:
a. GCA
b. Contractor
c. CSA
d. State Department
e. DGR

26. The contractual guidance provided for performing on classified contracts is found in:
a. Security Guidance Form
b. Security Specification Guide

c. Contract Security Classification Specification
d. Classified Work on Contracts Guidance
e. None of the above

27. Initially, who should the contractor notify in the event of challenge of classification?
a. CSA
b. CSO
c. GCA
d. GSA
e. CUR

28. Freight forwarders who take custody of classified material must have:
a. FCL
b. Adequate space
c. Proper security level storage capacity
d. a and b
e. a and c

29. What must the contractor do in cases of inadvertent release of classified material?
a. Determine clearance and access of holder
b. Provide written notice to those cleared for access of the proper classification
c. Determine if control of material has been lost
d. a and c
e. All of the above

30. Contractors should _____ during implementation of inspection procedures and bring significant problems to the _____.
a. Seek legal advice, FSO
b. Consult KMPs, CSA
c. Consult CSA, FSO
d. Consult FSO, CSA
e. Seek legal advice, CSA

31. Security reviews may not be conducted more than every _____ unless special circumstances exist.
a. 180 days
b. 26 weeks
c. 18 months
d. 24 months
e. None of the above-Depends on risk

32. Which positions must be cleared to the same access level of the FSO and FCL?
a. Senior management official and Insider Threat Program Senior Official
b. FSO and KMP's
c. CSO and senior management official CEO
d. ISSO and ISSM
e. KMP and ISSM

33. Reports of events impacting the FCL status should be submitted to:
a. FSO
b. GCA
c. CSA
d. GSA
e. a and c

34. Alternative Compensatory Control Measures include items identified as:
a. SECRET
b. CONFIDENTIAL
c. SAP
d. TOP SECRET
e. None of the Above

35. How many days from the date access to cryptographic information is not needed must an employee be debriefed?
a. 30 days
b. 90 days
c. 180 days
d. Two years
e. One year

36. Temporary PCLs apply to which of the following?
a. TOP SECRET
b. SECRET
c. CONFIDENTIAL
d. All of the above
e. b and c

37. If a company falls under FOCI, who is responsible for deciding that a limited entity eligibility is appropriate?
a. FSO
b. CSO
c. FBI
d. CSA
e. GCA

38. The NISP was established by:
a. Executive Order 12829
b. Executive Order 12333
c. Executive Order 13355
d. Executive Order 12356
e. Executive Order 12345

39. Written authorization of the _____ is required to transmit TOP SECRET information outside of the facility.
a. FSO
b. GCA
c. CSA
d. CSO
e. DCSA

40. Who can approve transmission of CNWDI classified outside of the facility?
a. GCA
b. CSA
c. FSO
d. CIA
e. FBI

41. Which of the following is true about information system passwords?
a. Protected in the same manner as information on the system
b. Protected at the same level as the information on the system
c. Changed in frequency to meet the level of risk assessed by CSA
d. a and c
e. All of the above

42. Which of the following constitute a primary reason(s) to reproduce TOP SECRET documents?
a. As required by operational needs
b. When directed by FSO
c. When directed by CSA
d. Contract is renewed
e. All of the above

43. Who is responsible as designated to receive TOP SECRET information?
a. TASCO
b. SAPCO
c. TSCO
d. ISSO
e. ITPSO

44. Concerning classified information, _____ must be destroyed as soon as practical after it has served its purpose.
a. Multiple copies
b. Original documents
c. Classified waste
d. a and b
e. All of the above

45. Storing information in a _____ may be necessary when other normal means are unsuitable or impractical:
a. Supplemental protection
b. Closed area
c. Open area
d. Restricted area
e. None of the above

46. For _____ material, only areas protected by IDS will qualify for open storage:
a. CONFIDENTIAL
b. TOP SECRET
c. SECRET
d. UNCLASSIFIED
e. a and c

47. When should TOP SECRET information be taken into accountability?
a. When transmitted outside of the facility
b. Immediately if not a finished document
c. Within 30 days of creation
d. Within 90 days of creation
b. None of the above

48. NATO has the following levels of security classification EXCEPT:
a. COSMIC TOP SECRET
b. NATO SECRET
c. NATO CONFIDENTIAL
d. NATO RESTRICTED
e. NATO TOP SECRET

49. What is the level of FCL a contractor facility must have to access NATO RESTRICTED?
a. TOP SECRET
b. SECRET
c. CONFIDENTIAL
d. RESTRICTED
e. None of the above

50. The wall construction in closed areas primary purpose is:
a. Offer resistance
b. Severe weather shelter
c. Provide evidence of unauthorized access
d. Protect from bomb blasts
e. a and c

51. Central monitoring stations may be located at which UL-listed location:
a. Military Operations Center
b. Emergency Operations Center
c. Cleared residential monitoring station

d. Uncleared commercial central station
e. All of the above

52. Central monitoring records shall be maintained indicating:
a. Time of the alarm
b. Names of security force detail responding
c. Time dispatched
d. Time of arrival
e. All of the above

53. The NISPOM also provides guidance for the classes of classified information including:
a. Restricted Data, COMSEC, CONFIDENTIAL, Unrestricted Data
b. Restricted Data, Formerly Restricted Data, Sensitive Compartmented Information and Special Access Program
c. COMSEC, Unrestricted Data, SECRET, Special Access Program
d. Restricted Data, CONFIDENTIAL, Sensitive Compartmented Information
e. Restricted Data, COMSEC, Sensitive Compartmented Information, Special Access Program

54. The Director Information Security Oversight Office, _____ and _____ the NISP implementation directive.
a. Measures and reads
b. Dictates and enforces
c. Issues and maintains
d. Installs and supervises
e. Writes and enforces

55. The overall classification shall be marked on which part of the document:
a. Top and bottom of outside cover
b. Title page
c. First page
d. All of the above
e. a and b

56. Which markings are appropriate for identifying the source of classification?
a. DERIVED FROM
b. DECLASSIFY ON
c. WRITTEN BY
d. All of the above
e. a and b

57. What must contractors determine and establish while hosting classified visits:
a. Identification of visitors
b. Appropriate PCL
c. Duration of meeting
d. Type of media used
e. a and b

58. Which of the following are part of "DoD Components"?
a. DOE
b. DOJ
c. FBI
d. CIA
e. Military Departments

59. Which of the following are types of international visit request?
a. Initial
b. Follow-up
c. Amendment
d. Special
e. Annual

60. If a contractor's FCL is terminated, how must classified documents be disposed of?
a. Return to GCA or as instructed by CSA
b. Return to CSA
c. Return to winning contractor
d. Destroy unless declassified
e. Ask for retention until FCL is reinstated

61. Who would provide guidance for the destruction of classified material?
a. GCA
b. CSA
c. FSO
d. GSA
e. CSO

62. Requests for government sponsored meetings should address all EXCEPT:
a. Dates of meeting
b. Location of meeting
c. Content of announcements
d. List of foreign representatives
e. Seating arrangements

63. Need to know for meetings are determined by:
a. Holder of classified material
b. Contractor
c. Authorizing agency
d. FSO
e. Visitor

64. For a classified contract, a _____ and a _____ shall be incorporated in the solicitations and subcontract.
a. Security requirements clause, Security Classification Guide
b. DD form 254, FCL
c. FCL, Security Classification Guide

d. Security requirements clause, Contract Security Classification Specification
e. DD Form 254, Security Classification Guide

65. The _____ shall be notified if the CSA discovers unsatisfactory security conditions in a subcontractor facility.
a. GCA
b. GSA
c. Prime contractor
d. Subcontractor
e. CSO

66. Which of the roles listed are responsibilities of the ISSM:
a. Accreditation/Approving Authority
b. Accredit information systems used to process classified information
c. Oversee development of facility IS Security Programs
d. Conduct risk management procedures based on contractor's facility
e. None of the above

67. Which E.O. provides information on marking classified email?
a. E.O. 12353
b. E.O. 13526
c. E.O. 11257
d. E.O. 13691
e. E.O. 12563

68. Confidential material may be transmitted outside of the U.S. by which means?
a. Registered mail through U.S. Military postal facilities
b. Cleared contractor employees
c. Designated courier
d. Cleared commercial carrier
e. All of the above

69. TOP SECRET material shall be stored in:
a. GSA approved security container
b. Approved vault
c. Approved closed area with supplemental controls
d. a and c
e. All of the above

70. Under SEAD and CSA guidance, what should contractors report?
a. Provide general information about protection of classified information
b. Provide reports to CSA, FBI and ISOO as required
c. Reports should be from the cleared employee to the CSA
d. When reports are classified, the Privacy Act does not apply to reports
e. All of the above

71. NSA is a government agency having classification jurisdiction over:
a. DOE
b. RD
c. COMSEC
d. FRD
e. DNI

72. How often should an inventory of TOP SECRET information be conducted?
a. Bi-annually
b. Annually
c. Semi-annually
d. Every 18 months
e. Every three years

73. Which level of classified information must follow a continuous receipt system?
a. CONFIDENTIAL
b. SECRET
c. TOP SECRET
d. b and c
e. All of the above

74. Working papers shall be marked the same as finished documents and at the same classification level. Which answer is correct concerning retention?
a. Transmitted within the facility
b. Retained for more than 30 days from creation for TOP SECRET
c. Retained for more than 180 days from creation for SECRET
d. Retained for more than 120 days from creation for SECRET
e. Retained for more than 120 days from creation for CONFIDENTIAL

75. The CSA can authorize up to _____ when factors preclude quicker alarm response time.
a. Thirty minutes
b. Fifteen minutes
c. Twenty minutes
d. One hour
e. What is reasonable to safeguard classified material

76. Which of the following can the CSA approve when no other alarm response options are available?
a. Response by neighborhood watch
b. Monitor by hidden camera
c. Guarded by working dogs
d. Installation of wire security
e. Response by cleared employee

77. Classified intelligence documents at a contractor facility shall be controlled according to NISPOM, with possible additional instructions from:
a. NRC
b. DNI

c. CSA
d. Intelligence Community Directives
e. FSO

78. The minimum investigation requirement for Q, TOP SECRET, and SCI levels is:
a. Non-critical sensitive
b. Moderate risk
c. Critical sensitive
d. Special risk
e. Polygraph

79. The minimum investigation requirement for SECRET is:
a. Non-critical sensitive
b. Critical sensitive
c. Special sensitive
d. High risk
e. Polygraph

80. Only contractors with access to RD and FRD can be trained and designated as _____ .
a. FRD Classifiers
b. RD derivative classification authority
c. NRC Classifiers
d. DOE Classifiers
e. DoD Classifiers

81. Cleared contractor employees must be briefed by the _____ prior to having access to CNWDI.
a. CSA
b. GCA
c. DOE
d. NRC
e. FSO

82. Accountability records for COSMIC TOP SECRET ATOMAL must be maintained for:
a. 10 years
b. Two years
c. Five years
d. Three years
e. Four years

83. Recommendations for the downgrading of NATO classified information should be forwarded to:
a. Originating activity
b. CSA
c. GSA
d. CUSR
e. FSCC

84. Under the insider threat plan, who is responsible to ensure that insider threat awareness is developed for IS users?
a. CSO
b. ISSO
c. FSO
d. FBI
e. ISSM

85. All of the following require accountability receipts EXCEPT:
a. NATO SECRET
b. NATO SECRET ATOMAL
c. COSMIC TOP SECRET
d. NATO CONFIDENTIAL
e. NATO CONFIDENTIAL ATOMAL

86. Which of the following characteristics is not used to describe a contractor?
a. Grantee
b. Certificate holder
c. Employee
d. Licensee
e. None of the above

87. An approved vault is constructed according to guidance in the NISPOM and approved by the:
a. CSA
b. GCA
c. FSO
d. ISSM
e. GSA

88. The structural integrity in closed areas should be ensured with:
a. Annual inspections
b. Monthly inspections
c. Contractor developed procedures
d. Inspections every three months
e. Whenever directed by CSA

89. Prior to having access to COMSEC, _____ must have a final PCL at the appropriate level for the material of the account.
a. FSO
b. COMSEC account manager
c. Alternate COMSEC account manager
d. All of the above
e. None of the above

90. When is it appropriate to mark an UNCLASSIFIED on classified documents and portions?
a. When document has been specifically reviewed to provide classification and those areas do not require classification

b. When document is stored with classified information
c. When document contains FOUO information
d. When document is provided to GCA as a deliverable
e. All of the above

91. Disclosure authorizations may manifest by which of the following?
a. Export license
b. Technical assistance agreement
c. Letter of authorization or exemption to export requirements
d. Manufacturing license agreement
e. All of the above

92. Which of the following is NOT required on a Visit Authorization Letter?
a. Contractors name
b. Level of PCL
c. Name of person to be visited
d. Contractors Social Security Number
e. Contractors telephone number

93. International visit requests include the following examples EXCEPT:
a. One-time
b. Recurring
c. Initial
d. Long-term
e. Emergency

94. The contractor should have approval of the _____ prior to requesting export authorization.
a. Contracts manager
b. GCA
c. CSA
d. FSO
e. None of the above

95. TOP SECRET information can be transmitted outside of the U.S by which means?
a. DCS
b. Escort with Top Secret Clearance
c. Authorized Courier
d. a and c
e. All of the above

96. Which of the following apply to conducting inspections?
a. All persons entering or exiting are subject to search
b. Limit searches to buildings where classified work is performed
c. Perform inspections on a random basis
d. Not necessary where possible access to classified material is remote
e. All of the above

97. Which are contractor inspection requirements required to reduce risk to classified information?
a. Perform inspections where unclassified work is performed
b. Perform inspections where classified work is performed
c. Post notices of inspections where possibility of access is remote
d. a and c
e. All of the above

98. Which actions are contractors required to take while enforcing perimeter controls?
a. No less than annually
b. No less than every 6 months
c. 18 months from authorization
d. Every three years
e. Only as required by GCA

99. May the CSA approve multiple stops while contract employee hand-carries classified material between countries?
a. Yes, if approved secure contractor storage is available
b. Never, only non-stop flights are authorized
c. Yes, if approved secure government storage is available
d. Yes, as long as classified never leaves courier sight
e. None of the above

100. Which of the following are appropriate portion markings found on classified documents?
a. SECRET, TOP SECRET, CONFIDENTIAL
b. S, TS, C
c. UNCLASSIFIED, TS, CONFIDENTIAL
d. FSO, TS, C, U
e. All of the above

101. Which change conditions are contractors required to report that may impact security clearance status?
a. Change of control of contractor
b. Change in contractor ownership
c. Significant stock transfers
d. a and c
e. All of the above

102. Sometimes classified material is created while working on a classified project. In many cases it will be destroyed as soon as possible. How should this information developed be marked?
a. No marking required
b. With the highest level of information in the project
c. MISCELLANEOUS CLASSIFIED
d. THIS INFORMATION IS MISCELLANEOUS
e. None of the above

103. It is the responsibility of_____ to indicate that information is "In Confidence".
a. CSA
b. Foreign government
c. FSO
d. GCA
e. CSO

104. The _____ serves as Executive Agent for the NISP.
a. Secretary of State
b. Department of the Army
c. Secretary of Defense
d. Department of Defense
e. Secretary of State

105. Which of the following is a requirement for closed area vault doors?
a. 8 inches thick
b. CSA approved
c. GCA approved
d. GSA approved
e. 4 inches thick

106. Which organization acts as CSA for the DoD?
a. Secretary of Energy
b. Director DCSA
c. Under Secretary of Defense for Intelligence & Security
d. Director of National Intelligence
e. Director of DOJ

107. Information is downgraded or declassified based on:
a. Political stabilization
b. Loss of sensitivity
c. Verification of public disclosure
d. Loss of application
e. Expiration of contract

108. Where should classification markings NOT appear on a classified document?
a. Front cover
b. Back cover
c. Title
d. Illustrations and charts
e. Sentences in a paragraph

109. Consultants can be cleared, however their performance on classified work is limited to:
a. The contractor facility unless in execution of authorized visits
b. Consultant home office with approved FCL
c. Consultant home office with contractor escort
d. Discretion of DD Form 254
e. All of the above

110. Which of the following are exempt from classification markings because of difficulty in marking?
a. Files
b. Folders
c. Email
d. Microfiche
e. None of the above

TEST 4

1. When requesting the retention of CONFIDENTIAL material beyond two years, the contractor can identify it by approximate number of documents and _____.
a. General subject matter
b. Author's name
c. Media type
d. Title
e. Date of creation

2. Pulverizing may only be used to destroy these kinds of products:
a. Paper
b. Metal
c. Plastic
d. Rubber
e. Computer

3. Which cleared employee, identified by position, ensures that insider threat awareness is developed for IS users?
a. CSA
b. GCA
c. FSO
d. ISSM
e. FBI

4. The Director of National Intelligence prescribes the sections of NISPOM that address _____ and _____ including _____.
a. Operations, intelligence sources, procurement
b. Intelligence sources, methods, SCI
c. SAP, intelligence sources, means
d. Organization, classification, procurement
e. Classification, dissemination, intelligence sources

5. The FSO shall complete training as considered appropriate by the:
a. CSA
b. GCA
c. GSA
d. NISPOM Training Annex
e. Senior ranking officer

6. A contractor should cooperate with Government agencies during official investigations. Which is a more likely scenario this cooperation could be demonstrated through?
a. Providing suitable place to conduct interview
b. Providing company car for offsite inspections
c. Providing computer access
d. a and b
e. All of the above

7. Which of the following determines a contractor's eligibility for access to classified information?
a. DISCO
b. Adjudication Agency
c. CSA
d. FSO
e. All of the above

8. Critical Nuclear Weapon Design Information is a _____ category of SECRET Restricted Data or TOP SECRET Restricted Data.
a. DOE
b. DoD
c. NRC
d. CSA
e. DOT

9. Employees sign certificates stating that they have been given a NATO security briefing. Certificates for NATO SECRET are maintained for:
a. Three years
b. Two years
c. Five years
d. Six years
e. Four years

10. For international transfers of classified material, follow-up action is sent through CSA if a signed receipt is not returned within:
a. 30 days
b. 15 days
c. 45 days
d. 3 days
e. 10 days

11. An emergency visit request is usually submitted within _____ calendar days of proposed visit.
a. 21
b. 4
c. 15
d. 7
e. 36

12. Which change conditions are contractors required to report that may impact security clearance status?
a. Change of control of contractor
b. Change in contractor ownership
c. Significant stock transfers
d. a and c
e. All of the above

13. Which is a responsibility of the Secretary of Energy?
a. Authority for procedures for information classified under AEA
b. Authority over access to information classified under AEA
c. Authority over portions pertaining to information classified as RD
d. Authority over portions pertaining to information classified as FRD
e. All of the above

14. All of the following should be documented on the SF 86 EXCEPT:
a. Deceased parents
b. Deceased father-in-law
c. Deceased mother-in-law
d. Deceased cousins
e. All should be reported

15. How long will the FSO maintain a copy of an employee's SF 86?
a. Five years
b. Ten years
c. Until clearance is granted or denied
d. Until employee terminates employment
e. 180 days

16. Refresher security training for cleared employees must be completed at least:
a. Every six months
b. Annually
c. Quarterly
d. Every three months
e. Upon discretion of FSO

17. Central monitoring stations shall be required to:
a. Monitor each alarmed area
b. Have video surveillance
c. Have remote access to doors
d. Report hourly to guards
e. Call periodically during storms

18. Subcontracted guards must be under a classified contract with which of the following?
a. GCA, CSA
b. CSA, DCSA
c. Cleared contractor facility
d. Monitoring station, installing alarm company
e. All of the above

19. Contractors who paraphrase classified information are making _____ decisions:
a. Reasons for classification
b. Security Classification Guidance
c. Derivative classification
d. Classification
e. Classified document

20. A U.S. contractor's ability to access classified information stored abroad is the responsibility of:
a. GCA
b. U.S. Government
c. CSA
d. State Department
e. DGR

21. U.S. RESTRICTED AND FORMERLY RESTRICTED Data is marked all EXCEPT:
a. COSMIC TOP SECRET ATOMAL
b. NATO RESTRICTED ATOMAL
c. NATO CONFIDENTIAL ATOMAL
d. NATO SECRET ATOMAL
e. None of the above

22. Which entity is required to review and revise the Contract Security Classification Specification when change occurs?
a. CSO
b. GCA
c. CSA
d. FSO
e. GSA

23. Which are appropriate page markings for a document classified at the SECRET level?
a. SECRET, TOP SECRET, SENSITIVE, CONFIDENTIAL
b. CONFIDENTIAL, SECRET, UNCLASSIFIED
c. CONFIDENTIAL, FOUO, TOP SECRET
d. UNCLASSIFIED, FOUO, SENSITIVE
e. All of the above

24. During UNCLASSIFIED visits by foreign nationals, it is a _____ responsibility to ensure export authorizations are obtained.
a. GCA
b. Contractor
c. CSA
d. State Department
e. DGR

25. Which organization acts as CSA for the DoD?
a. Secretary of Energy
b. Director DCSA

c. Under Secretary of Defense for Intelligence & Security
d. Director of National Intelligence
e. Director of DOJ

26. Which of the following duties may a designated ISSO perform?
a. Certify that system security plan is implemented
b. Recommend self-inspection corrective actions
c. Develop information system security programs
d. Command security resources
e. Grant IATOs

27. TOP SECRET control officials shall be designated to _____, _____, _____TOP SECRET information.
a. Transmit, maintain access and accountability records for, and receive
b. Create, classify, brief, document
c. Receive, create, classify, disseminate
d. Request, assign, account, disseminate
e. Receive, transmit, classify, document

28. Classified working papers generated by contractors in preparation of finished project shall be:
a. Dated when created
b. Marked with overall classification and annotated "WORKING PAPERS"
c. Stored separately from finished documents
d. a and b
e. All of the above

29. What frequency of security reviews shall be conducted on cleared facilities?
a. Periodic
b. CSA determines
c. Annual
d. Semi-Annual
e. Monthly

30. Contractors are required to report:
a. Events that have an impact on FCLs
b. Events that have an impact on PCLs
c. Events that have an impact on ability to safeguard classified information
d. All of the above
e. b and c

31. When should a contractor sign a receipt for transmission of CONFIDENTIAL material?
a. Not a requirement
b. Always a requirement
c. If receipt has errors
d. a and c
e. All of the above

32. Information classified as SECRET can be transmitted outside of facility by all means EXCEPT:
a. Defense Courier Service, if authorized by GCA
b. U.S. Postal Service Registered Mail
c. U.S. Postal Service Priority Mail
d. Cleared commercial carrier
e. Cleared commercial messenger service

33. What should the FSO do with original, signed copies of the SF 86 and the Authorization for Release of Information and Records before access eligibility is granted or denied?
a. Send to GCA
b. Send to FBI
c. Retain
d. Return to applicant
e. All of the above

34. Which of the following is NOT an insider threat training topic for all cleared personnel?
a. Detecting insider threats
b. Reporting insider threats
c. Applicable legal policies
d. Counterintelligence reporting requirements
e. Threat behavior indicators

35. All the following provide an appropriate proof of U.S. citizenship EXCEPT:
a. Driver's license
b. Birth Certificate
c. Expired Passport
d. DD Form 1966
e. Current Passport

36. Announcements of meetings shall be _____ and require government approval.
a. FOUO
b. SECRET
c. CONFIDENTIAL
d. UNCLASSIFIED
e. TOP SECRET

37. Which of the following is NOT true concerning classified information in meetings?
a. Can be presented orally
b. Can be presented visually
c. Can be distributed to attendees
d. Attendees must turn in classified notes
e. Classified notes will be disseminated per NISPOM

38. When wrapping classified material for shipment, the _____ cannot go on the outer label:
a. Classification level
b. Office code letter
c. Office code number

d. Directions for routing
e. Facility name

39. All of the following must be included in the authorization letter for hand carrying classified material on a commercial aircraft EXCEPT:
a. Traveler's Social Security Number
b. Description of traveler's ID
c. Description of material being carried
d. Identify points of departure, destination, and known transfer point
e. Location and telephone number of CSA

40. Contractors shall limit the number of PCL requests to:
a. One third of the company
b. KMPs and direct reports
c. That which is necessary to operate efficiently
d. Meet future requirements for classified contracts
e. That which is specifically outlined on the DD Form 254

41. The NISP applies to which agency(s)?
a. NRC
b. CIA
c. NRA
d. Secretary of Defense
e. NSC

42. Among other requirements, the destruction records for TOP SECRET must contain the _____ and be kept for _____.
a. Date of destruction, two years
b. SSN of destroyer, two years
c. Name of destroyer, one year
d. ID material destroyed, one year
e. Date of Classification, five years

43. Which is not a training requirement for the Insider Threat Program personnel as described in NISPOM?
a. Security Fundamentals
b. Insider threat response procedures
c. Safety considerations
d. Privacy Policies
e. Consequences of misusing collected records and data

44. Which types of door locking devices are approved protecting stored SECRET and CONFIDENTIAL information?

a. Key operated lock
b. Hand print reader
c. Deadbolt lock
d. Swipe card reader
e. All of the above

45. Which E.O. provides guidance for safeguarding USG classified information?

a. E.O. 12353
b. E.O. 12829
c. E.O. 11257
d. E.O. 13691
e. E.O. 12563

46. Which E.O. provides information on marking classified email?

a. E.O. 12353
b. E.O. 13526
c. E.O. 11257
d. E.O. 13691
e. E.O. 12563

47. Which response force could the CSA approve as a last resort?

a. Cleared contractor employees
b. Subcontracted guard force
c. Military police
d. Civil police
e. Proprietary security force

48. Need to know is generally based on:

a. Level of clearance
b. Block 13 of DD Form 254
c. Security Classification Guide
d. Contractual relationship
e. As determined by CSA

49. Who has security oversight of contract employees who are long term visitors at government installations?

a. GCA
b. CSA
c. Contractor
d. Host installation
e. CSO

50. 23. Which of the following are part of "DoD Components"?

a. DOE
b. DOJ

c. FBI
d. CIA
e. Military departments

51. Which of the following characteristics is not used to describe a contractor?
a. Grantee
b. Certificate holder
c. Licensee
d. Employee
e. None of the above

52. The NISP was established by:
a. Executive Order 12829
b. Executive Order 12333
c. Executive Order 13355
d. Executive Order 12356
e. Executive Order 12345

53. CONFIDENTIAL material may be stored the same as higher classification levels EXCEPT:
a. Supplemental controls are not necessary
b. Storage in steel filing cabinets do not apply to the October 1 2012 requirement
c. Storage cabinets do not have to be GSA approved
d. None of the above
e. All of the above

54. All of the following shall be transferred internationally through the CUSR Registry EXCEPT:
a. NATO SECRET
b. NATO SECRET ATOMAL
c. COSMIT TOP SECRET
d. NATO CONFIDENTIAL
e. NATO CONFIDENTIAL ATOMAL

55. Which of the following are appropriate portion markings found on classified documents?
a. SECRET, TOP SECRET, CONFIDENTIAL
b. S, TS, C
c. UNCLASSIFIED, TS, CONFIDENTIAL
d. FSO, TS, C, U
e. All of the above

56. Consultants can be cleared, however their performance on classified work is limited to:
a. The contractor facility unless in execution of authorized visits
b. Consultant home office with approved FCL
c. Consultant home office with contractor escort
d. Discretion of DD Form 254
e. All of the above

57. Contractors shall submit reports to the:
a. FSO and DIA
b. FBI and CSA
c. CSO and DIA
d. FBI and CIA
e. CIA and DIA

58. The government approves _____ before contractors can conduct a classified meeting at a contractor facility?
a. Attendees
b. Announcements
c. Security arrangements
d. All of the above
e. None of the above

59. What actions must CSA take if FCL cannot be granted in sufficient time to qualify subcontractor for participating in current procurement actions?
a. Immediately cease processing
b. Continue processing for 90 days
c. Continue processing for 120 days
d. Continue processing
e. None of the above

60. A contractor is any educational, industrial, commercial or any other entity that has been granted a(n) _____ by the _____.
a. PCL, GSA
b. FCL, GCA
c. FCL, CSA
d. PCL, CSA
e. FCL, FSO

61. The _____ determines the duties of the ISSO:
a. CSA
b. GCA
c. FSO
d. ISSM
e. FBI

62. Selection of appropriate protection measures should be based on:
a. Reaccreditation
b. System implementation
c. Re-evaluation of accreditation
d. Assessment of risk and conditions
e. Annual review

63. If retention of classified documents under an expired contract is desired for longer than the 2-year period, who is the approval authority?
a. GCA
b. CSA
c. FSO
d. FBI
e. CSO

64. What is the primary disposition of classified documents where retention has not been authorized?
a. Disseminate to winning bid contractor
b. Destroy unless declassified
c. Maintain on site
d. a and c
e. None of the above

65. Need to know is generally based on:
a. Level of clearance
b. Block 13 of DD Form 254
c. Security Classification Guide
d. Contractual relationship
e. As determined by CSA

66. Who receives reports of duplicate audits?
a. CSA
b. ISSM
c. FSO
d. GCA
e. ISOO

67. TOP SECRET material shall be stored in:
a. GSA approved security container
b. Approved vault
c. Approved closed area with supplemental controls
d. a and c
e. All of the above

68. CSA approval to extend alarm response time may be annotated in the:
a. Standard Security Procedures
b. Alarm certificate
c. Monitoring station
d. Alarm System Description Form
e. Guard check list

69. In the normal course of business contractors may disclose classified material to cleared individuals in all cases EXCEPT:
a. Company employees
b. MFO
c. Subcontractors
d. DoD activities
e. Between Federal Agencies

70. When can authorized contractors disclose classified information to federal or state courts?
a. When instructed by the agency having jurisdiction over the information
b. When instructed by the attorney representing the U.S.
c. When instructed by the GCA
d. a and b
e. All of the above

71. When downgrading or declassifying notification is contrary to markings shown, the contractor will remark to identify change and include:
a. Identify authority, date of action, identity of approving CSA
b. Date of action, identity of authority, position of person taking action
c. Identity of authority, date of notification, identity of approving CSA
d. Identity of authority, date of notification, identity of contractor taking action
e. None of the above

72. What are the required elements of a derivatively classified document?
a. "DECLASSIFY ON"
b. "CLASSIFIED BY"
c. "DERIVED FROM"
d. None of the above
e. All of the above

73. Open bin storage is not allowed for:
a. TOP SECRET
b. SECRET
c. CONFIDENTIAL
d. UNCLASSIFIED
e. a and b

74. The contractor shall document IS protection procedures in the _____.
a. SSP
b. IS Certification Report
c. Master SPP
d. SPP
e. Security Classification Guide

75. Three types of investigations and reports contractors should send to the CSA include:
a. Initial, secondary and final
b. Preliminary, initial and final

c. Initial, follow-up and final
d. Preliminary, initial and follow-up
e. Annual, refresher and final

76. What are some actions that a company may take during the FCL process?
a. Provide list of employees, submit SF 86 applications, process KMPs for PCLs
b. Execute CSA forms, process KMPs for PCLs, appoint U.S. citizen as FSO
c. Execute CSA forms, submit SF 86 applications, provide list of employees
d. Provide list of employees, process KMPs for PCLs, appoint U.S. citizen as FSO
e. Provide list of employees, submit SF 86 applications, process KMPs for PCLs

77. All of the following require accountability receipts EXCEPT:
a. NATO SECRET
b. NATO SECRET ATOMAL
c. COSMIC TOP SECRET
d. NATO CONFIDENTIAL
e. NATO CONFIDENTIAL ATOMAL

78. The only time RD and FRD shall be disclosed to international governments is:
a. When the US contractor and foreign government have an agreement
b. When the CSA and contractor have an agreement
c. When the United States and participating governments sign an agreement
d. When the United States and all entities bid on information
e. When the US contractor and all entities sign treaty

79. The investigative tier standards for CONFIDENTIAL clearance investigations include:
a. Moderate risk
b. High risk
c. Special Sensitive
d. Critical Sensitive
e. Polygraph

80. Which agencies determine which classified information to remove from the RD category to make it FRD?
a. DOE and DoD
b. DOE and NRC
c. DoD and NRC
d. DoD and CSA
e. CSA and NRC

81. COSMIC TOP SECRET documents shall have reference numbers on:
a. Each page of the document
b. The front and back covers
c. On the first page
d. On the title and first pages
e. On the appendix page

82. DTIC is responsible for remarking classification levels of documents after downgrading or declassification. The remarking occurs on all the following EXCEPT the:
a. Complete document
b. Front and back covers
c. Title page
d. First page
e. Back pages

83. Where should classification information NOT appear on a classified document?
a. Each page
b. Each paragraph
c. Title
d. Illustrations and charts
e. All of the above

84. In order to protect fragile intelligence resources and methods, _____ is responsible for parts of NISPOM that address SCI.
a. NSA
b. GCA
c. DNI
d. CSA
e. GSA

85. Temporary TOP SECRET FCLs or PCLs are valid for access to COMSEC at the ____ and ____ levels.
a. SECRET, TOP SECRET
b. TOP SECRET, CONFIDENTIAL
c. CONFIDENTIAL, FOUO
d. SECRET, FOUO
e. CONFIDENTIAL, SECRET

86. The COR establishes the COMSEC account and notifies the:
a. CSA
b. GCA
c. FSO
d. NSA
e. DIA

87. Contractors maintain TOP SECRET reproduction records for _____ years.
a. Two years
b. One year
c. Five years
d. Ten years
e. None of the above

88. Contractors are authorized to retain classified material received under contract for a period of_____ after completion of contract.
a. One year
b. Two years
c. Five years
d. 180 days
e. 90 days

90. Which of the following is NOT true of the General Security Agreement between countries?
a. Limits use each governments information
b. Restricts third party transfers
c. Does not commit governments to share classified
d. Constitutes authority to release classified material to government
e. Satisfies the eligibility requirements for foreign governments to protect U.S. classified defense articles

91. The _____ has oversight of contract security requirements on behalf of foreign governments.
a. CSA
b. GCA
c. FSO
d. Contract manager
e. Embassy

92. All U.S. classified information must be transferred to the recipient government through its:
a. DGR
b. GCA
c. COR
d. CSA
e. FSO

93. Which of the following types of carriers does NOT meet requirements for international transfer of classified material?
a. Chartered or owned by a NATO country
b. Chartered or owned by recipient country
c. Chartered by the U.S.
d. Under U.S. Registry
e. Authorized by DSA of the GCA and security authorities of involved governments

94. The highest level of classified information that can be hand carried outside the U.S. is:
a. CONFIDENTIAL
b. FOUO
c. SECRET
d. TOPSECRET
e. RESTRICTED

95. A U.S. company is under FOCI when:
a. A foreign interest creates job announcements in the U.S.
b. A foreign interest exercises power that may result in unauthorized disclosure of classified information
c. A U.S. company markets product oversees
d. A foreign interests visit cleared facilities
e. A foreign involvement causes stock prices to fall

96. According to the Certificate Pertaining to Foreign Interests (SF 328), indicators that require reporting to the CSA include:
a. Organization owns 10% or more of total revenue or net income from any single foreign person
b. Five percent or more of voting securities held in shares that do not identify the beneficial owner
c. Organization owns 10 percent or more of any foreign interest
d. Organization has three or more contracts with a foreign person
e. KMPs make frequent visits to foreign countries

97. The dispatching company security officer must provide the receiving security officer with _____ advance notice of the couriers expected date and time of arrival.
a. 48 hours
b. 72 hours
c. 24 work hours
d. 12 hours
e. 86 hours

98. All of the following are portion markings that one might find on foreign classified information EXCEPT:
a. TOP SECRET
b. SECRET
c. REGISTERED
d. RESTRICTED or In Confidence
e. UNCLASSIFIED

99. Which of the following are considered a CSA?
a. Department of Defense
b. Central Intelligence Agency
c. Department of Energy
d. The Nuclear Regulatory Commission
e. All of the above

100. Reference numbers on US originated NATO documents must be on _____ of a document:
a. Each page of the document
b. The front and back covers
c. The first page
d. The title and first pages
e. The appendix page

101. Which of the following actions are required before a prime contractor can release information to a subcontractor?
a. Determine security requirements of the contract
b. Ensure subcontractor has sufficient employees to safeguard classified information
c. Grant subcontractor necessary clearance
d. Evaluate closed area construction
e. Develop subcontractor access control requirements

102. What method of justification should a contractor submit to attend a classified meeting?
a. Provide information on the classified contract involved
b. Cite the clearance level
c. Give company CAGE code
d. Submit job position
e. List qualifications

103. What should contractors ensure their derivative classifiers accomplish?
a. Be an original classifier
b. Complete derivative classifier training
c. Complete a waiver if derivative classifier training is not available
d. Complete FSO certification training
e. a and c

104. The NISPOM also applies to classified information not released under a license, _____, grant, or certificate.
a. TAA
b. Contract
c. License
d. Scope
e. Registration

105. Executive Order 12829 requires heads of agencies to enter into agreement with:
a. FSO
b. Foreign governments
c. Secretary of Defense
d. Department of Labor
e. Department of Energy

106. How might a cleared contractor mark unclassified training material to simulate SECRET?
a. UNCLASSIFIED SAMPLE
b. SECRET FOR TRAINING PURPOSES
c. SECRET FOR TRAINING ONLY
d. SECRET FOR TRAINING, OTHERWISE UNCLASSIFIED
e. All of the above

107. Which is not a training requirement for the Insider Threat Program Senior Official as described in NISPOM?
a. Counterintelligence Fundamentals
b. ITAR Fundamentals
c. Security Fundamentals
d. Insider threat response procedures
e. Civil liberties policies

108. Initial Security Briefings should include which of the following?
a. Counterintelligence awareness
b. Cybersecurity awareness
c. Insider threat awareness
d. a and c
e. All of the above

109. Derivative classifiers should be identified on derivatively classified documents by which means?
a. Name
b. Position
c. Identifier
d. a and b
e. All of the above

110. _____ Security Agreements are negotiated with various foreign governments.
a. Multi-force
b. Bi-lateral
c. Uni-lateral
d. Multi-lateral
e. Bi-layered

PRACTICE TEST ANSWERS

We have provided test answers in long and short versions.

Long Version

If you want to compare your answers and continue your study, review the long version answers. This version provides the answer, plus references the NISPOM location to find your answers.

Short Version

Looking for a quick answer? Just go to the short version and see what the answer is.

TEST 1 ANSWERS-LONG VERSION

1. _____ Security Agreements are negotiated with various foreign governments.
a. Multi-force
b. Bi-lateral (NISPOM 117.19)
c. Uni-lateral
d. Multi-lateral
e. Bi-layered

2. The _____ retains authority over access to intelligence methods and sources.
a. DNI (NISPOM 117.23)
b. FBI
c. DCSA
d. CIA
e. SECDEF

3. The NISPOM also applies to classified information not released under a license, _____, grant, or certificate.
a. TAA
b. Contract (NISPOM 117.2)
c. License
d. Scope
e. Registration

4. Which of the following are part of "DoD Components"?
a. Combatant Commands (NISPOM 117.2)
b. Department of Justice
c. FBI
d. CIA
e. All of the above

5. Who is responsible to advise in the development of the Contract Security Classification Specification?
a. GCA
b. CSA
c. Contractor (NISPOM 117.13)
d. DCSA
e. GCO

6. Contractors should train all _____ including outside of the U.S. of obligation to protect classified information.
a. Cleared employees (NISPOM 117.7)
b. Company employees
c. Visitors
d. Temporary employees
e. All of the above

7. Which of the following characteristics is not used to describe a contractor?
a. Grantee
b. Certificate holder
c. Employee (NISPOM 117.3)
d. Licensee
e. None of the above

8. Contractors shall submit reports to the:
a. FSO and DIA
b. FBI and CSA (NISPOM 117.8)
c. CSO and DIA
d. FBI and CIA
e. CIA and DIA

9. Disclosure of U.S. Information to Foreign Governments is guided by the:
a. CSA
b. GCA (NISPOM 117.19)
c. COR
d. ITAR
e. Exports Agreements

10. To which security clearance level is required for access to NATO RESTRICTED information?
a. TOP SECRET
b. SECRET
c. CONFIDENTIAL
d. RESTRICTED
e. None of the above (NISPOM 117.19)

11. Which of the following are eligibility requirements a company must meet before it can be processed for an FCL?
a. The company must be an organization of at least twenty-five people
b. The company must have a desire for classified access
c. The company must have a reputation for integrity (NISPOM 117.9)
d. The company must make its bottom line for three consecutive quarters
e. The company is the only entity that can perform the work

12. When can a contractor provide classified access to another contractor?
a. Furtherance of contract (NISPOM 117.15)
b. Furtherance of business development
c. When directed by FSO
d. When directed by CSA
e. Just as long as other contractor is cleared

13. Unless restricted by the GCA, SECRET material may be reproduced as follows EXCEPT:
a. In performance of a prime contract
b. In performance of subcontract in furtherance of prime contract
c. Upon closure of contract (32 CFR 2001.45)

d. In preparation of patent applications
e. In preparation of bid to a Federal Agency

14. International visit requests include the following examples EXCEPT:
a. One-time
b. Recurring
c. Initial (NISPOM 117.19)
d. Long-term
e. Emergency

15. Which are contractor inspection requirements required to reduce risk to classified information?
a. Perform inspections where unclassified work is performed
b. Perform inspections where classified work is performed (NISPOM 117.15)
c. Post notices of inspections where possibility of access is remote
d. a and c
e. All of the above

16. Violations of export control regulations subjecting classified information to possible compromise by foreign nationals shall be reported to the:
a. GCA
b. Contractor
c. CSA (NISPOM 117.19)
d. State Department
e. DGR

17. When sending a report for changes in cleared KMPs, what information must be included:
a. Level of clearance and when cleared, date and place of birth, social security numbers, citizenship, status of exclusion from access (NISPOM 117.8)
b. Special accesses, citizenship, date of employment, date of birth and current address, date of facility clearance
c. Date of employment, clearance level and date, citizenship, social security number, status of exclusion from access
d. Special accesses, date and place of birth, social security number, date of employment, status of exclusion from access
e. Special access, level of clearance, citizenship

18. Which entities must be cleared to the same access level as the FCL?
a. Senior management official, FSO, KMP
b. FSO, KMP, ITPSO
c. FSO, senior management official, ITPSO (NISPOM 117.7)
d. FSO, KMPs, all security personnel
e. All of the above

19. A contractor's information security system should use a _____ based approach to protect against unauthorized disclosure of classified information.
a. Confidentiality
b. Risk (NISPOM 117.18)
c. Threat
d. Vulnerability
e. Availability

20. The ISs protection should be documented in the:
a. System Security Plan (NISPOM 117.18)
b. Standard Operating Procedure
c. Insider Threat Plan
d. Program Protection Plan
e. All of the above

21. Reports submitted to the CSA include:
a. Sabotage
b. Espionage
c. Adverse Information (NISPOM 117.8)
d. Acts of terrorism
e. None of the above

22. Risk Management Framework includes which of the following steps:
a. Categorized information processed on an IS
b. Assess and determine extent of security control implementation
c. Inventory IS components
d. a and b (DSS Assessment and Authorization Process Manual)
e. All of the above

23. _____ have been used widely as set of best practices for authorizing and assessing information systems.
a. DoD 5220.22-M
b. DoDI 5200.44
c. NIST Risk Management Framework (DSS Assessment and Authorization Process Manual)
d. CNSS I 1253
e. CNSS D 504

24. What are the appropriate steps to take in DISS when a cleared employee no longer needs a clearance but will remain with the company?
a. Admin Debrief
b. Debrief from access, separate from DISS
c. Separate from DISS, out process
d. Out process only
e. Separate from DISS only

25. What level of classified information should be maintained under an information management system?
a. CONFIDENTIAL
b. SECRET

c. TOP SECRET
d. b and c
e. All of the above (NISPOM 117.15)

26. You must include information about all of the following EXCEPT on the SF86:
a. Parents
b. Cousins
c. Brothers
d. Sisters
e. Spouses

27. When must fingerprints be submitted?
a. For initial investigations and Periodic Review
b. For initial investigations only
c. For PR's only
d. At the completion of investigation
e. Never

28. Which E.O. provides guidance for safeguarding USG classified information?
a. E.O. 12353
b. E.O. 12829 (NISPOM 117.1)
c. E.O. 11257
d. E.O. 13691
e. E.O. 12563

29. Consultants can be cleared, however their performance on classified work is limited to:
a. The contractor facility unless in execution of authorized visits (NISPOM 117.10)
b. Consultant home office with approved FCL
c. Consultant home office with contractor escort
d. Discretion of DD Form 254
e. All of the above

30. Some of the methods to mitigate or negate risks of foreign ownership or control include:
a. Board Resolution
b. Security Control Agreement
c. Special Security Agreement
d. a and c
e. All of the above (NISPOM 117.11)

31. Required training under the Initial Security Briefing will include which of the following:
a. Threat awareness
b. Reporting obligations
c. Cleared Facility Orientation
d. a and b (NISPOM 117.12)
e. All of the above

32. All contractor requests for interpretations of the NISPOM shall be forwarded through the _____ to the _____.

a. FBI, CSA
b. DCSA, CSA
c. DCSA, FBI
d. CSO only
e. CSA only (NISPOM 117.7)

33. FSO qualifications include being a _____ and _____.

a. U.S. Citizen, cleared as part of FCL (NISPOM 117.9)
b. U.S. Citizen, exempt from clearance
c. U.S. Citizen, certified as ISP
d. U.S. Citizen, attended college
e. U.S. Citizen, cleared to SCI

34. When a contractor challenges a classification, if no written answer is provided within 60 days, the contractor should request help from the _____.

a. CSA (NISPOM 117.13)
b. GSA
c. GCA
d. FBI
e. FSO

35. Which organization acts as CSA for the DoD?

a. Secretary of Energy
b. Under Secretary of Defense for Intelligence & Security (NISPOM 117.6)
c. Director DCSA
d. Director of National Intelligence
e. Director of DOJ

36. All attendees of meetings shall possess _____and _____.

a. Clearance, need to know (NISPOM 117.16)
b. Clearance, ID card
c. Authorized tablet, pen
d. VAL, authorization
e. Clearance, authorization

37. Which of the following actions are required before the prime contractor may release or disclose classified information to a subcontractor?

a. Determine clearance status (NISPOM 117.17)
b. Determine size of company
c. Determine capability to perform work on time
d. Determine type of business
e. Determine location of work performed

38. Where initial response teams consist of uncleared employees, which of the following response times apply?

a. 72 hours
b. 48 hours
c. A reasonable amount of time (NISPOM 117.15)
d. 30 days
e. 45 days

39. A record of TOP SECRET material must be made when material is:

a. Completed as a finished document
b. Retained for more than 180 days of creation
c. Transmitted outside of the facility
d. None of the above
e. All of the above (NISPOM 117.15)

40. SECRET material shall be stored in which of the following scenarios:

a. GSA approved security container
b. Approved vault
c. Closed areas (Supplemental controls not necessary)
d. a and b (CFR 2001.43)
e. All of the above

41. Concerning a government contractor monitoring station with a response team cleared at the SECRET level, how many guards are required to respond to an alarm?

a. At least two when at least one guard is cleared
b. The amount sufficient to immediately investigate each alarm (NISPOM 117.15)
c. At least five when at least one guard is cleared
d. At least four when at least one guard is cleared
e. At least three when at least one guard is cleared

42. Who determines need to know at classified meetings?

a. GCA
b. Contract monitor
c. Individual disclosing information (NISPOM 117.16)
d. Visiting individuals
e. FSA

43. The structural integrity in closed areas should be ensured with:

a. Annual inspections
b. Monthly inspections
c. Contractor developed procedures (NISPOM 117.15)
d. Inspections every three months
e. Whenever directed by CSA

44. Which E.O. provides guidance for safeguarding USG classified information?
a. E.O. 12353
b. E.O. 12829 (NISPOM 117.1)
c. E.O. 11257
d. E.O. 13691
e. E.O. 12563

45. How many days from the date access to cryptographic information is not needed must an employee be debriefed?
a. 30 days
b. 90 days (NISPOM 117.21)
c. 180 days
d. Two years
e. One year

46. TOP SECRET information can be transmitted by which of the following methods within the U.S. and its territories:
a. Defense Courier Service, if authorized by GCA (32 CFR 2001.46)
b. A courier cleared at the SECRET level
c. By electrical means over FSO approved secured communication devices
d. By government vehicle
e. By U.S. Postal Service Registered Mail

47. SECRET information can be transmitted by which of the following means:
a. Registered mail
b. Cleared commercial carrier
c. As authorized by the GCA
d. Commercial company approved by CSA
e. All of the above (32 CFR 2001.46)

48. Couriers shall ensure all EXCEPT:
a. Information remains under constant protection
b. Information remains under continuous protection
c. They possess authorization to store classified in hotel safe (32 CFR 2001.46)
d. Locked briefcase may serve as outer layer
e. None of the above

50. The foreign government designation of RESTRICTED should be given what level of protection in the U. S. where bilateral security agreements exist:
a. SECRET
b. TOP SECRET
c. CONFIDENTIAL (NISPOM 117.14)
d. UNCLASSIFIED
e. FOUO

51. May the CSA approve multiple stops while a contract employee hand-carries classified between countries?
a. Yes, if approved secure contractor storage is available
b. Never, only non-stop flights are authorized
c. Yes, if approved secure government storage is available (NISPOM 117.19)
d. Yes, as long as classified never leaves courier sight
e. None of the above

52. Which of the following are types of international visit request?
a. Initial
b. Follow-up
c. Amendment (NISPOM 117.19)
d. Special
e. Annual

53. If retention of classified documents under an expired contract is desired for longer than the two year period, who is the approval authority?
a. GCA (NISPOM 117.15)
b. CSA
c. FSO
d. FBI
e. CSO

54. What is the primary disposition of classified documents where retention has not been authorized?
a. Disseminate to winning bid contractor
b. Destroy unless declassified (NISPOM 117.15)
c. Maintain on site
d. a and c
e. None of the above

55. Destruction records are required for:
a. TOP SECRET (NISPOM 117.15)
b. SECRET
c. CONFIDENTIAL
d. a and b
e. All of the above

56. Construction in closed areas should be built of material that:
a. Prevents opening by magnetic pulse
b. Prevents opening by shotgun blast
c. Provides evidence of unauthorized access (32 CFR 2001.53)
d. Protects from bomb blasts
e. a and c

57. Vents with openings greater than 96 inches and over _____inches at smallest measurement shall be protected.

a. 2
b. 6 (32 CFR 2001.53)
c. 9
d. 10
e. 18

58. How many employees must be working at a SECRET cleared central station?

a. Two
b. Five
c. Enough to sufficiently monitor each cleared contractors alarmed area (NISPOM 117.15)
d. One as long as there is a quick reaction team
e. None of the above

59. Which of the following resources are authorized to investigate alarms at a cleared contractor facility?

a. Local police force
b. FBI
c. Fire department
d. Subcontracted guards (NISPOM 117.15)
e. Military police

60. The requirement for on time response for alarms is:

a. 75%
b. 85%
c. 90%
d. 65%
e. 80% (NISPOM 117.15)

61. Persons attending classified meetings must have the proper _____:

a. Clearance and need to know (NISPOM 117.16)
b. Clearance and authority
c. Authority and need to know
d. Access and reporting authority
e. Accountability and authenticity

62. Repairs of approved containers include which of the following procedures:

a. Damaged or altered parts are replaced with manufacturer's replacement
b. Damaged or altered parts replaced with identical cannibalized parts
c. Damaged or altered parts are repaired with other than approved methods if storing SECRET material under supplemental controls until October 1, 2012
d. According to FED STD 809 (NISPOM 117.15)
e. All of the above

63. Which statement is true of government officials visiting a contractor facility?

a. They must relinquish control of their work product
b. Classified work product must be handled according to GCA regulations

c. Government employees are not required to relinquish work product unless it is classified
d. Presents appropriate credentials (NISPOM 117.16)
e. None of the above

64. An information system's security efforts should include a baseline set of _______, _______, and technical controls.
a. Management, Operational (NISPOM 117.18)
b. Visual, Audible
c. Standardized, Authentic
d. Risk Based, Authentic
e. Availability, Integrity

65. Which of the following is true about information system passwords
a. Protected in the same manner as information on the system
b. Protected at the same level as the information on the system
c. Changed in frequency to meet the level of risk assessed by CSA
d. a and c
e. All of the above (NISPOM 117.18)

66. Who approves security changes to an IS?
a. ISSM
b. GCA
c. FSO
d. ISSO
e. CSA (NISPOM 117.18)

67. Under SEAD and CSA guidance, what should contractors report?
a. Provide general information about protection of classified information
b. Provide reports to CSA, FBI and ISOO as required (NISPOM 117.8)
c. Reports should be from the cleared employee to the CSA
d. When reports are classified, the Privacy Act does not apply to reports
e. All of the above

68. Storing information in a _____ may be necessary when other normal means are unsuitable or impractical:
a. Supplemental protection
b. Closed area (NISPOM 117.15)
c. Open area
d. Restricted area
e. None of the above

69. Reference numbers on US originated NATO documents must be on _____ of a document:
a. Each page of the document
b. The front and back covers
c. The first page (NISPOM 117.19)
d. The title and first pages
e. The appendix page

70. Recommendations for the declassification of NATO classified information should be forwarded to:
a. Originating activity
b. CSA
c. CISSP
d. CUSR (NISPOM 117.19)
e. FSCC

71. Verification of a meeting, the attendee's identity is verified by official photographic identification such as:
a. Passport
b. Contractor ID
c. Military ID
d. CAC card
e. All of the above (NISPOM 117.16)

72. If a prospective subcontractor does not have the appropriate FCL, or safeguarding capability, the _____ shall request the CSA of the _____ to initiate the necessary action.
a. Subcontractor, prime contractor
b. Prime contractor, GCA
c. Prime contractor, subcontractor (NISPOM 117.17)
d. GCA, prime contractor
e. GCA, subcontractor

73. A contractor is any _____ entity that has been granted an FCL by the CSA
a. Educational
b. Industrial
c. Commercial
d. Other
e. All of the above (NISPOM 117.3)

74. If a cleared facility hosts a government sponsored classified meeting, which of the following must be approved by the government?
a. Menu
b. Seating order
c. Announcements (NISPOM 117.16)
d. Slide show background
e. Dress code

75. When taking action to downgrade classified information, the contractor must seek guidance from:
a. GSA
b. CSA
c. GCA (NISPOM 117.13)
d. FBI
e. CSO

76. Which of the following apply to end of day security checks?
a. Perform checks at the close of each working day

b. Perform checks at end of last shift in which classified material was removed for use
c. Not necessary during continuing 24 hour operations
d. a and c
e. All of the above (NISPOM 117.15)

77. An original Contract Security Classification Specification shall be included with each:
a. RFQ
b. RFP
c. IFB
d. Other solicitation
e. All of the above (NISPOM 117.17)

78. If an ISSO is designated to conduct self-inspections, they should provide results to the:
a. GCA
b. FSO
c. CSA
d. ISSM (NISPOM 117.18)
e. GSA

79. An employee may be processed for a PCL when the ______ determines access is essential.
a. Contractor (NISPOM 117.17)
b. CSO
c. GCA
d. CSA
e. ISSM

80. Which E.O. provides information on marking classified email?
a. E.O. 12353
b. E.O. 13526 (NISPOM 117.12)
c. E.O. 11257
d. E.O. 13691
e. E.O. 12563

81. Concerning meetings, the _____ shall create security requirements and get the _____ approval.
a. Contractor, FSO
b. Contractor, CSA
c. FSO, CSA
d. CSA, authorizing agency
e. Contractor, authorizing agency (NISPOM 117.16)

82. Which is a responsibility of the Secretary of Energy?
a. Authority for procedures for information classified under AEA
b. Authority over access to information classified under AEA
c. Authority over portions pertaining to information classified as RD
d. Authority over portions pertaining to information classified as FRD
e. All of the above (NISPOM 117.6)

83. Who has responsibility for assessing information systems?
a. CSA and Contractor (NISPOM 117.18)
b. FSO and ISSM
c. ISSM and ISSO
d. ISSO and GCA
e. CSA and GCA

84. Which change conditions are contractors required to report that may impact security clearance status?
a. Change of control of contractor
b. Change in contractor ownership
c. Significant stock transfers
d. a and c
e. All of the above (NISPOM 117.7)

85. Which of the following apply to conducting inspections?
a. All persons entering or exiting are subject to search
b. Limit searches to buildings where classified work is performed
c. Perform inspections on a random basis
d. Not necessary where possible access to classified material is remote
e. All of the above (NISPOM 117.15)

86. Contractors shall conduct the self-inspections at iterations consistent with:
a. Risk management principles (NISPOM 117.7)
b. DCSA inspection dates
c. FSO determination
d. Previous results
e. All of the above

87. Under the certification and accreditation, the old term certification now crosswalks to the RMF term _____.
a. Authorization
b. System Security plan
c. Security Controls
d. Assessment (DSS Assessment and Authorization Process Manual)
e. Impact

88. What should contractors ensure their derivative classifiers accomplish?
a. Be an original classifier
b. Complete derivative classifier training (NISPOM 117.12)
c. Complete a waiver if derivative classifier training is not available
d. Complete FSO certification training
e. a and c

89. Which of the following are appropriate portion markings found on classified documents?
a. SECRET, TOP SECRET, CONFIDENTIAL
b. S, TS, C (Marking Classified National Security Information)

c. UNCLASSIFIED, TS, CONFIDENTIAL
d. FSO, TS, C, U
e. All of the above

90. The _____ has authority pertaining to access to intelligence methods and sources.
a. NSA
b. DoD
c. DNI (NISPOM 117.6)
d. DOA
e. GCA

91. Contractors shall report all unauthorized disclosure concerning RD and FRD to the:
a. DOE
b. NRC
c. CSA (NISPOM 117.23)
d. GCA
e. FSO

92. The minimum investigation requirements for TOP SECRET Q is:
a. Investigative tier appropriate for moderate risk positions
b. investigative tier appropriate for non-critical sensitive positions
c. investigative tier appropriate for high risk positions (NISPOM 117.10)
d. a and b
e. None of the above

93. The minimum investigation requirements for CONFIDENTIAL PCL is:
a. Investigative tier appropriate for moderate risk positions (NISPOM 117.10)
b. Investigative tier appropriate for high risk positions
c. Investigative tier appropriate for high critical sensitive positions
d. Investigative tier appropriate for special sensitive positions
e. Investigative tier appropriate for critical sensitive positions

94. Challenges to improperly classified RD/FRD documents should be addressed through the:
a. GCA (NISPOM 117.20)
b. CSA
c. DOE
d. DoD
e. NRC

95. Contractors shall not disclose CNWDI to subcontractors without approval of the:
a. CSA
b. GCA (NISPOM 117.20)
c. DOE
d. NRC
e. FSO

96. For government sponsored classified meetings at contractor facilities, who is responsible for assuming security jurisdiction?
a. The cleared contractor
b. The subcontracted security force
c. Authorizing government agency (NISPOM 117.16)
d. Proprietary guard force
e. CSA

97. The _____ shall develop the security measures and obtain the _____ approval.
a. Contractor, FSO
b. Contractor, CSA
c. FSO, CSA
d. CSA, authorizing agency
e. Contractor, authorizing agency (NISPOM 117.16)

98. NATO visit records must be kept for:
a. Two years
b. Three years (NISPOM 117.19)
c. One year
d. 180 days
e. Four years

99. The NISP was established by:
a. Executive Order 12829 (NISPOM 117.1)
b. Executive Order 12333
c. Executive Order 13355
d. Executive Order 12356
e. Executive Order 12345

100. Which of the following are NOT listed as Proscribed Information?
a. TOP SECRET
b. SECRET (NISPOM 117.3)
c. COMSEC
d. RD
e. SAP

101. TOP SECRET material shall be stored in a(n):
a. GSA approved security container
b. Approved vault
c. Approved closed area with supplemental controls
d. a and c
e. All of the above (32 CFR 2001.43)

102. Before COMSEC can be released to a contractor, the _____ must verify with the _____ that appropriate procedures are in place.
a. CSA, FSO
b. GCA, FSO

c. NSA, FSO
d. GCA, CSA (NISPOM 117.21)
e. DIA, NSA

103. The _____ establishes the COMSEC account and notifies the CSA.
a. COR (NISPOM 117.21)
b. GCA
c. FSO
d. NSA
e. DIA

104. Requirements for access to CRYPTO include the following EXCEPT:
a. U.S. citizenship
b. Valid need-to-know
c. CI scope polygraph (NISPOM 117.21)
d. Appropriately cleared with a final security clearance
e. Appropriately briefed

105. The NISPOM prescribes the _____, _____, and other _____ to prevent unauthorized disclosure of classified information.
a. Standards, values, restrictions
b. Requirements, restrictions, safeguards (NISPOM 117.1)
c. Date, time, measures
d. Content, procedures, standards
e. Date, procedures, safeguards

106. The _____ has been designated Executive Agent for the NISP by the President.
a. National Security Council
b. Secretary of State
c. Director of National Intelligence
d. Director of the CIA
e. Secretary of Defense (NISPOM 117.6)

107. _____ Security Agreements are negotiated with various foreign governments.
a. Multi-force
b. Bi-lateral (NISPOM 117.19)
c. Uni-lateral
d. Multi-lateral
e. Bi-layered

108. Foreign nationals can participate in classified gatherings if authorized by the head of the _____ authorizing the meeting.
a. U.S. Government Agency (NISPOM 117.19)
b. FSO
c. CSO
d. Contractor
e. None of the above

109. The failure of a foreign entity to provide classification guidance should be reported to the:
a. Contracts manager
b. GCA
c. CSA (NISPOM 117.19)
d. FSO
e. COR

110. Reproduction of foreign TOP SECRET information requires approval of the:
a. GCA
b. Originating Government (NISPOM 1117.19)
c. CSA
d. State Department
e. None of the above

TEST 2 Answers-Long Version

1. The NISP was established by:
a. Executive Order 12829 (NISPOM 117.1)
b. Executive Order 12333
c. Executive Order 13355
d. Executive Order 12356
e. Executive Order 12345

2. An employee with a privileged user account can perform which of the following functions?
a. System Control
b. System Monitoring
c. Data Transfer
d. Functions general users are not authorized to perform
e. All of the above (DSS Assessment and Authorization Process Manual)

3. General and privileged users should receive which of the following training?
a. Threat awareness training
b. Insider threat training
c. Risks associated with user activities
d. NISP based responsibilities
e. All of the above (NISPOM 117.12)

4. Contractors performing work on federal installations shall safeguard classified information according to procedures of:
a. NISPOM
b. Block 13 of DD Form 254
c. Host Installation or Agency (NISPOM 117.7)
d. CSA
e. CSO

5. Contractors shall establish procedures for _____notification after death or incapacitation.
a. CSA (NISPOM 117.7)
b. GCA
c. Next of kin
d. FSO
e. FBI

6. Reports submitted to the _____ involve espionage, terrorism and sabotage.
a. CIA
b. FSO
c. CSA
d. ISSM
e. FBI (NISPOM 117.8)

7. Consultants can be cleared, however their performance on classified work is limited to:
a. The contractor facility unless in execution of authorized visits (NISPOM 117.10)
b. Consultant home office with approved FCL
c. Consultant home office with contractor escort
d. Discretion of DD Form 254
e. All of the above

8. Contractors are permitted to implement downgrading or declassification upon guidance or notification from?
a. CSA
b. CSO
c. GSA
d. GCA (NISPOM 117.13)
e. None of the above

9. International visit requests include the following examples EXCEPT:
a. One-time
b. Recurring
c. Initial (NISPOM 117.19)
d. Long-term
e. Emergency

10. Selections for types of visit on the visit request form include:
a. Initial
b. Follow-up
c. Amendment (NISPOM 117.19)
d. Special
e. Annual

11. Which positions must be cleared to the same access level of the FCL?
a. Senior management official and Insider Threat Program Senior Official
b. FSO and KMP's
c. FSO and senior management official
d. a and c (NISPOM 117.9)
e. b and c

12. An authorization is required _____ a contractor makes an export proposal to a foreign interest that involves release of U.S. classified information.
a. When
b. Before (NISPOM 117.19)
c. After
d. Unless
e. None of the above

13. The _____ shall identify the recipient government's DGR and appoint a U.S. DGR.
a. COR
b. CSA (NISPOM 117.19)
c. FSO
d. GCA
e. State Department

14. Which of the following are appropriate portion markings found on classified documents?
a. SECRET, TOP SECRET, CONFIDENTIAL
b. S, TS, C (Marking Classified National Security Information)
c. UNCLASSIFIED, TS, CONFIDENTIAL
d. FSO, TS, C, U
e. All of the above

15. The moderate risk, non-critical sensitive tier is required for access to classified information up to which levels?
a. CONFIDENTIAL, L, and SECRET PCLs (NISPOM 117.10)
b. TOPSECRET, Q, and SCI access
c. TOP SECRET
d. a and c
e. SECRET only

16. The Secretary of Energy or the Chairman of the Nuclear Regulatory Commission are responsible for prescribing procedure for:
a. Portions of this rule that pertain to information under DNI programs
b. Portions of this rule that pertain to information under DOE programs
c. Portions of this rule that pertain to information under NRC programs (NISPOM 117.6)
d. Portions of this rule that pertain to information under SAP programs
e. None of the above

17. The _____ will address complaints and suggestions with respect to the administration of the NISP.
a. Secretary of Defense
b. Director of FBI
c. Defense Security Services
d. Director of ISOO (NISPOM 117.6)
e. Cognizant Security Agency

18. Which of the following is not a risk designation for security clearances?
a. Positions designated as moderate risk
b. Positions designated as medium risk (NISPOM 117.6)
c. Positions designated as high risk
d. Positions designated as low risk
e. None of the above

19. For a Tier 3 investigation you must provide work experience for the past _____ years.
a. Ten
b. Twenty
c. Seven
d. Five
e. Three

20. How long does a security clearance remain in effect?
a. Forever
b. five years for TS
c. ten years for S
d. As long as employed and expected to require access to classified information
e. b and c

21. Who conducts security clearance investigations for the DoD?
a. Each cleared contractor is required to pay for investigations
b. FBI
c. DCSA
d. OPM
e. CAF

22. How many days must the employee begin work after a PCL is granted according to the commitment for employment?
a. 60 days
b. 45 days (NISPOM 117.10)
c. 180 days
d. 90 days
e. 56 days

23. Which of the following are part of "DoD Components"?
a. DOE
b. DOJ
c. FBI
d. CIA
e. Military Departments (NISPOM 117.2)

24. From whom would a contractor receive a facility clearance assurance for a foreign entity?
a. CSA
b. Cleared contractor
c. GCA
d. Sponsoring government's security authority (NISPOM 117.19)
e. Department of State

25. Derivative Classification includes:
a. Incorporated classified information
b. Restated classified information
c. Generate classified information in a new form

d. All of the above (NISPOM 117.3)
e. b and c

26. To whom does a contractor initially submit classification challenges?
a. GCA (NISPOM 117.13)
b. CSA
c. FSO
d. FBI
e. GSA

27. Required security training and briefing titles include:
a. Initial security briefings, refresher, annual briefings
b. Initial security briefings, annual, debriefings
c. Initial security briefings, Insider threat training, CUI training (NISPOM 117.12)
d. Annual, refresher, initial security briefings
e. Initial security briefings, annual, refresher

28. Contractors shall conduct formal self inspections at intervals consistent with:
a. At least annually and according to risk management principles (NISPOM 117.7)
b. DCSA inspection dates
c. FSO determination
d. Previous results
e. All of the above

29. All classified information and material should be marked to clearly convey:
a. Level of classification
b. Portions that reveal classified
c. Portions that contain classified
d. Period of time protection is required
e. All of the above (NISPOM 117.14)

30. NATO has the following levels of security classification EXCEPT:
a. COSMIC TOP SECRET
b. NATO SECRET
c. NATO CONFIDENTIAL
d. NATO RESTRICTED
e. NATO TOP SECRET (NISPOM 117.19)

31. In situations of classified information inadvertently released as UNCLASSIFIED, the contractor's notice shall be classified _____ unless it contains information for higher classification.
a. UNCLASSIFIED
b. FOR OFFICIAL USE ONLY
c. SECRET
d. TOP SECRET
e. CONFIDENTIAL (NISPOM 117.14)

32. Which of the following contract information requires GCA approval before release to the public?
a. Release of unclassified information on a classified contract (NISPOM 117.17)
b. The fact that a contract has been received
c. The method of contract
d. The fact that a contract is negotiated
e. Whether or not contract requires hiring or terminating of employees

33. Which are contractor inspection requirements required to reduce risk to classified information?
a. Perform inspections where unclassified work is performed
b. Perform inspections where classified work is performed (NISPOM 117.15)
c. Post notices of inspections where possibility of access is remote
d. a and c
e. All of the above

34. Contractors shall maintain a record of destruction of SECRET material for _____ years.
a. Two years
b. One year
c. Five years
d. Thirty days
e. None of the above (NISPOM 117.19)

35. Controlling access to classified material in an open area during working hours is an example of:
a. Supplemental protection
b. Establishing a closed area
c. Establishing an open area
d. Establishing a restricted area (NISPOM 117.3)
e. None of the above

36. For NATO accountability records, titles should not contain:
a. Reference number
b. Short title
c. Classification level
d. Classified information (NISPOM 117.19)
e. All of the above

37. CONFIDENTIAL is approved for transmission by which of the following means?
a. U.S. Postal Service Priority Mail
b. U.S. Postal Service First Class Mail
c. Any commercial overnight delivery company
d. U.S. Postal Service Certified Mail (32 CFR 2001.46)
e. All of the above

38. Authorization in writing by the _____ is required for transmission of TOP SECRET outside of a facility while the electrical transmission means over _______ approved secured communications security circuits.
a. CSA, GSA
b. CSA, FSO

c. FSO, DOT
d. CSA, DOT
e. GCA, CSA (32 CFR 2001.46)

39. What should be provided in an escort's written instructions prior to shipping classified information?
a. Receipt procedures
b. Means of transportation
c. Emergency communication procedures
d. Route to be used
e. All of the above (NISPOM 117.15)

40. When is a company under FOCI eligible for a security clearance?
a. When FSO has submitted final report
b. Once security measures to mitigate or negate FOCI are established (NISPOM 117.9)
c. When FSO completes OPSEC report
d. Upon completion of foreign interest visit
e. Upon completion of initial report

41. If required, the FSO Program Management Course should be complete within _____ of appointment to the position of FSO.
a. 30 days
b. 90 days
c. Three months
d. Six months (NISPOM 117.12)
e. One year

42. Which government agency has jurisdiction over RD?
a. NSA
b. FRD
c. DNI
d. CSA
e. DOE (NISPOM 117.23)

43. How often must contractors review security programs?
a. On a recurring basis (NISPOM 117.7)
b. Monthly
c. Within 180 days of accountability
d. Before contract end
e. Annually during inventory

44. Receipts must be provided for which level of classified material?
a. SECRET (32 CFR 2001.26)
b. CONFIDENTIAL
c. UNCLASSIFIED
d. a and b
e. All of the above

45. Working papers shall be marked the same as finished documents and at the same classification level. Which answer is correct concerning retention?

a. Transmitted within the facility
b. Retained for more than 30 days from creation for TOP SECRET
c. Retained for more than 180 days from creation for SECRET (NISPOM 117.15)
d. Retained for more than 120 days from creation for SECRET
e. Retained for more than 120 days from creation for CONFIDENTIAL

46. Classified material may be destroyed by which of the following methods?

a. Mutilation
b. Chemical decomposition
c. Pulverization
d. Melting
e. All of the above (32 CFR 2001.47)

47. Which E.O. provides information on marking classified email?

a. E.O. 12353
b. E.O. 13526 (NISPOM 117.12)
c. E.O. 11257
d. E.O. 13691
e. E.O. 12563

48. Which of the following apply to conducting inspections?

a. All persons entering or exiting are subject to search
b. Limit searches to buildings where classified work is performed
c. Perform inspections on a random basis
d. Not necessary where possible access to classified material is remote
e. All of the above (NISPOM 117.15)

49. The contractor shall forward the names of employees who shall serve as COMSEC and alternate COMSEC account managers to the _____.

a. GCA
b. FSO
c. CSA (NISPOM 117.21)
d. NSA
e. COR

50. Contractors must obtain written approval from the _____ before subcontracting COMSEC work.

a. COR
b. NSA
c. DIA
d. CSA
e. GCA (NISPOM 117.21)

51. Government representatives serving in an official capacity may visit a contractor facility in which of the following circumstances?
a. Official capacity as inspectors
b. When presenting appropriate identification
c. Official capacity as auditors
d. Official capacity as investigators
e. All of the above (NISPOM 117.16)

52. ______ issues protective measures and guidance on protection of ISs.
a. GCA
b. ISSO
c. FSO
d. CSA (NISPOM 117.18)
e. NISPOM

53. Where initial response teams consist of uncleared employees, which of the following response times apply?
a. 72 hours
b. 48 hours
c. A reasonable amount of time (NISPOM 117.15)
d. 30 days
e. 45 days

54. Which of the following is true about information system passwords
a. Protected in the same manner as information on the system
b. Protected at the same level as the information on the system
c. Changed in frequency to meet the level of risk assessed by CSA
d. a and c
e. All of the above (NISPOM 117.18)

55. When sending a report for changes in cleared KMPs, which information must be included?
a. Level of clearance and when cleared, date and place of birth, social security numbers, citizenship, status of exclusion from access (NISPOM 117.8)
b. Special accesses, citizenship, date of employment, date of birth and current address, date of facility clearance
c. Date of employment, clearance level and date, citizenship, social security number, status of exclusion from access
d. Special accesses, date and place of birth, social security number, date of employment, status of exclusion from access
e. Special access, level of clearance, citizenship

56. The system security program should be delegated by the:
a. FSO
b. ISSO
c. CSA
d. SSM (NISPOM 117.18)
e. System user

57. Which of the following are types of international visit request?
a. Initial
b. Follow-up
c. Amendment (NISPOM 117.19)
d. Special
e. Annual

58. If a cleared facility hosts a government sponsored classified meeting, which of the following must be approved by the government?
a. Menu
b. Seating order
c. Announcements (NISPOM 117.16)
d. Slide show background
e. Dress code

59. Which organization approves use of IDS?
a. FSO
b. CSO
c. CSA (NISPOM 117.15)
d. GCA
e. GSA

60. Response times for investigating alarms shall not exceed:
a. Thirty minutes
b. Fifteen minutes
c. Twenty minutes
d. One hour (NISPOM 117.15)
e. What is reasonable to safeguard classified material

61. All attendees of classified meetings shall possess _____ and _____.
a. Clearance, need to know (NISPOM 117.16)
b. Clearance, ID card
c. Authorized tablet, pen
d. VAL, authorization
e. Clearance, authorization

62. What is one of the required actions necessary before a prime contractor may release or disclose classified information to a subcontractor?
a. Determine clearance status (NISPOM 117.17)
b. Determine size of company
c. Determine capability to perform work on time
d. Determine type of business
e. Determine location of work performed

63. Construction in closed areas should be built of material that:
a. Prevents opening by magnetic pulse
b. Prevents opening by shotgun blast
c. Provides evidence of unauthorized access (32 CFR 2001.53)
d. Protects from bomb blasts
e. a and c

64. Vents with openings greater than 96 inches and over ______inches at smallest measurement shall be protected.
a. 2
b. 6 (32 CFR 2001.53)
c. 9
d. 10
e. 18

65. Contractors must obtain ______ approval before installing Intrusion Detection Systems.
a. CSS
b. CSA (NISPOM 117.15)
c. GCA
d. GSA
e. DIA

66. Which of the following reflect the bilateral security agreement?
a. Requires each government to provide different degrees of protection
b. Provides restrictions for third party transfers (NISPOM 117.19)
c. Allows for unlimited use of information and third party transfers
d. Doesn't meet requirements found in the Arms Export Control Act
e. None of the above

67. Open bin storage is not allowed for:
a. TOP SECRET (32 CFR 2001.43)
b. SECRET
c. CONFIDENTIAL
d. UNCLASSIFIED
e. a and b

68. What level of classified information should be maintained under an information management system?
a. CONFIDENTIAL
b. SECRET
c. TOP SECRET
d. b and c
e. All of the above (NISPOM 117.15)

69. Which organization ensures FSOs receive briefings for special categories of information?
a. CSA (NISPOM 117.12)
b. GCA
c. ISSM
d. FSO
e. GSA

70. Who is responsible for providing initial security briefings to the FSO?
a. DSSA
b. FSO
c. CSO
d. GCA
e. CSA (NISPOM 117.12)

71. A contractor is any educational, industrial, commercial, other entity that has been granted an FCL by the:
a. GCA
b. DIA
c. CIA
d. GSA
e. CSA (NISPOM 117.3)

72. The _____ chooses controls, the _____provides set of security controls, and _____ acknowledges risk.
a. Contractor, CSA, USG (NISPOM 117.18)
b. ISSO, ISSM, CSA
c. ISSO, GCA, CSA
d. CSA, Contractor, GSA
e. ISSO, GSA, GCA

73. Need to know is generally based on:
a. Level of clearance
b. Block 13 of DD Form 254
c. Security Classification Guide
d. Contractual relationship (NISPOM 117.16)
e. As determined by CSA

74. Which entities must be cleared to the same access level as the FCL?
a. Senior management official, FSO, KMP
b. FSO, KMP, ITPSO
c. FSO, senior management official, ITPSO (NISPOM 117.7)
d. FSO, KMPs, all security personnel
e. All of the above

75. The duties of the ISSM include:
a. Have oversight of the development of the contractor's IS program (NISPOM 117.18)
b. Serve as the Authorization to Operate Authority
c. Issue protective measure guidance

d. Designate security control profiles
e. Provide guidelines for operational and technical controls

76. Which of the following apply to end of day security checks?
a. Perform checks at the close of each working day
b. Perform checks at end of last shift in which classified material was removed for use
c. Not necessary during continuing 24 hour operations
d. a and c
e. All of the above (NISPOM 117.15)

77. The NISPOM requires the frequency of classified visits be:
a. No more than one per week
b. Unlimited as long as FSO's keep a log
c. Unlimited due to Freedom of Information Act
d. Kept to a minimum (NISPOM 117.16)
e. Determined by amount of classified contracts

78. Continuous evaluation uses _____ and ______ in the assessment of security clearance eligibility.
a. records checks, business rules (NISPOM 117.3)
b. Certification, Accreditation
c. investigations, questionnaires
d. Analysis, Prioritization
e. Authorization, Accreditation

79. TOP SECRET information should be made a permanent record when:
a. A temporary product
b. Retained for 90 days or fewer
c. Transmitted outside of the facility (NISPOM 117.15)
d. Retained for 120 days or fewer
e. None of the above

80. Which organization has the ability to authorize information systems used to process classified information?
a. CSA (NISPOM 117.18)
b. GSA
c. ISSM
d. ISSO
e. GCA

81. Storing information in a _____ may be necessary when other normal means are unsuitable or impractical:
a. Supplemental protection
b. Closed area (NISPOM 117.15)
c. Open area
d. Restricted area
e. None of the above

82. Which organization certifies that an information system incorporates a protection program that includes CSA required controls?
a. CSA
b. GSA
c. Contractor (NISPOM 117.18)
d. None of the above
e. All of the above

83. The management of classified IS primarily concerns prevention of:
a. Loss of confidentiality
b. Loss of integrity
c. Loss of availability
d. Unauthorized disclosure of classified information (NISPOM 117.18)
e. None of the above

84. If a contractor believes information to be classified when it was not originally identified as classified, the contractor should:
a. Hold the information as unclassified until determination is made
b. Return to the customer through same method as delivered
c. Protect as classified and return to proper agency (NISPOM 117.13)
d. Mark as classified and store with similar classified items
e. Destroy the item

85. Which of the following should be included in an information system's security program?
a. Risk reducing policies and procedures
b. Adequate information security plans for classified data on IS
c. A methodology for implementing mitigations addressing IS policy gaps
d. Ability to evaluate IS security controls
e. Plans and procedures to assess, report, isolate, and contain data spills and compromises, to include sanitization and recovery methods (NISPOM 117.18)

86. What should contractors ensure their derivative classifiers accomplish?
a. Be an original classifier
b. Complete derivative classifier training (NISPOM 117.12)
c. Complete a waiver if derivative classifier training is not available
d. Complete FSO certification training
e. a and c

87. Which are processes of the RMF?
a. Prepare
b. Categorize
c. Select
d. a and b
e. All of the above (DSS Assessment and Authorization Process Manual)

88. Which of the following can grant access to RD and FRD?
a. DOE
b. NRC
c. DoD
d. NASA
e. All of the above (NISPOM 117.23)

89. Alternative Compensatory Control Measures include items identified as:
a. SECRET
b. CONFIDENTIAL
c. SAP (NISPOM 117.23)
d. TOP SECRET
e. None of the above

90. Only contractors with ______ may classify or upgrade matter containing RD and FRD.
a. FRD Classifiers
b. RD derivative classification authority (NISPOM 117.23)
c. NRC Classifiers
d. DOE Classifiers
e. DoD Classifiers

91. _____ is a DoD category of TOP SECRET Restricted Data or SECRET Restricted Data that reveals operation of components of a thermonuclear bomb.
a. CNWDI (NISPOM 117.23)
b. FRD
c. RD
d. NATO
e. EWNDI

92. Water repellent papers shall be destroyed by:
a. Shredding
b. Burning
c. Disintegration
d. Pulping
e. a, b, or c (32 CFR 2001.47)

93. Working papers shall be marked the same as finished documents and at the same classification level. Which answer is correct concerning retention?
a. Transmitted within the facility
b. Retained for more than 30 days from creation for TOP SECRET
c. Retained for more than 180 days from creation for SECRET (NISPOM 117.15)
d. Retained for more than 120 days from creation for SECRET
e. Retained for more than 120 days from creation for CONFIDENTIAL

94. Employees shall sign a certificate stating that they have been given a NATO security briefing. Certificates for NATO CONFIDENTIAL must be maintained for:
a. Three years
b. Two years (NISPOM 117.23)
c. Five years
d. Seven years
e. Four years

95. Suspected loss or compromise of classified information must be reported to the:
a. FBI
b. GSA
c. CSA (NISPOM 117.8)
d. ISSO
e. SGM

96. Which organization acts as CSA for the DoD?
a. Secretary of Energy
b. Under Secretary of Defense for Intelligence & Security (NISPOM 117.6)
c. Director DCSA
d. Director of National Intelligence
e. Director of DOJ

97. Under SEAD and CSA guidance, what should contractors report?
a. Provide general information about protection of classified information
b. Provide reports to CSA, FBI and ISOO as required (NISPOM 117.8)
c. Reports should be from the cleared employee to the CSA
d. When reports are classified, the Privacy Act does not apply to reports
e. All of the above

98. How many days from the date access to cryptographic information is not needed must an employee be debriefed?
a. 30 days
b. 90 days (NISPOM 117.21)
c. 180 days
d. Two years
e. One year

99. For international transfers, if the courier doesn't arrive within _____ hours of anticipated delivery time, the receiving security officer must notify the dispatching security officer.
a. 36 hours
b. 10 hours
c. 24 hours
d. 8 hours (NISPOM 117.19)
e. 4 hours

101. All of the following require destruction certificates EXCEPT:
a. NATO SECRET
b. NATO SECRET ATOMAL
c. COSMIC TOP SECRET
d. NATO CONFIDENTIAL (NISPOM 117.19)
e. NATO CONFIDENTIAL ATOMAL

102. Which of the following characteristics is not used to describe a contractor?
a. Grantee
b. Certificate holder
c. Employee (NISPOM 117.3)
d. None of the above
e. Licensee

103. Which E.O. provides information on marking classified email?
a. E.O. 12353
b. E.O. 13526 (NISPOM 117.12)
c. E.O. 11257
d. E.O. 13691
e. E.O. 12563

104. Which agency has classification authority and can authorize release of COMSEC information to a foreign person?
a. NSA (NISPOM 117.15)
b. DIA
c. CIA
d. DoD
e. DOE

105. The FSO, COMSEC and alternate COMSEC account managers shall be briefed by the _____ or their designee.
a. Government representative (NISPOM 117.12)
b. KMP
c. FSO
d. COR
e. Outgoing custodian

106. Initial reports submitted to the FBI must be followed up by:
a. Telephone reports and submitted to CSA in writing
b. Written reports and a copy submitted to CSA (NISPOM 117.8)
c. Face to face reports and submitted to CSA in writing
d. a and b
e. All of the above

107. The structural integrity in closed areas should be ensured with:
a. Annual inspections
b. Monthly inspections
c. Contractor developed procedures (NISPOM 117.15)
d. Inspections every three months
e. Whenever directed by CSA

108. The _____ provides the security classification guides.
a. FSO
b. CSA
c. GCA (NISPOM 117.13)
d. DoD
e. Secretary of Defense

109. Which change conditions are contractors required to report that may impact security clearance status?
a. Change of control of contractor
b. Change in contractor ownership
c. Significant stock transfers
d. a and c
e. All of the above (NISPOM 117.7)

110. Which is not a reportable event that impacts the status of PCLs and FCLs?
a. Contractors did not attend Prevention of Sexual Harassment Training (NISPOM 117.8)
b. Employee is an insider threat
c. Security containers are often left unlocked and unattended
d. Classified laptop was stolen from a government vehicle
e. Classified notebook was stolen from a privately owned vehicle

TEST 3 ANSWERS-LONG VERSION

1. The _____ or _____ may inspect and monitor contractor, licensee, grantee, and certificate holder programs and facilities.

a. Secretary of Defense, NRC
b. Secretary of Energy, Secretary of Defense
c. Secretary of Energy, FBI
d. Secretary of Defense, DCSA
e. Secretary of Energy, Chairman of NRC (NISPOM 117.6)

2. The requirement for heads of agencies to enter into agreement with the Secretary of Defense as the Executive agent for the NISP is:
a. 32 CFR part 2004 (NISPOM 117.7)
b. Executive order 12958
c. NISPOM
d. Executive Order 12929
e. ITAR

3. The CSA shall forward the names of cleared and briefed employees who shall serve as FSO, COMSEC and alternate COMSEC custodians to the:
a. COR, GCA (NISPOM 117.21)
b. NSA
c. DoD
d. DIA
e. DOE

4. "The transfer of technical data, articles, and _____ to foreign persons…constitutes an export".
a. Services (NISPOM 117.19)
b. Books
c. Tools
d. Weapons
e. Aircraft

5. Which E.O. provides guidance for safeguarding USG classified information?
a. E.O. 12353
b. E.O. 12829 (NISPOM 117.1)
c. E.O. 11257
d. E.O. 13691
e. E.O. 12563

6. Requests for NISPOM interpretation by contractors on U.S. Government installations should be sent to the _____ via the Commander.
a. CSO
b. President
c. GCA
d. Translator
e. CSA (NISPOM 117.7)

7. SPP's shall be certified in writing by the _____ to the ____ that the plan is implemented.
a. CSA, CSO
b. FBI, FSO
c. FSO, CSA (NISPOM 117.18)
d. CSA, SECDEF
e. CSA, FBI

8. Which is a responsibility of the Secretary of Energy?
a. Authority for procedures for information classified under AEA
b. Authority over access to information classified under AEA
c. Authority over portions pertaining to information classified as RD
d. Authority over portions pertaining to information classified as FRD
e. All of the above (NISPOM 117.6)

9. _____ shall provide security training to cleared employees and advise them of obligations to protect classified information.
a. CSA
b. DSSA
c. CSO
d. FSO
e. Contractors (NISPOM 117.12)

10. Contractors shall submit corrective actions taken against an employee to the CSA when it is determined that the employee is responsible for a security violation and _____ is evident:
a. The violation involved a deliberate disregard of security requirements (NISPOM 117.8)
b. The violation was just a one-time incident without violation of procedure
c. The violation was not deliberate and did not involve a pattern of negligence
d. The violator was not remorseful
e. The violation happened in spite of the excellent care in the handling of classified material

11. How long must a contractor maintain original CSA designated forms?
a. Duration of the contract and DD Form 254
b. Two years
c. For the FCL duration (NISPOM 117.9)
d. Five years
e. When contractor has significant change in status

12. Concerning IS privileges, all users shall:
a. Have access to IS control
b. Have access to IS monitoring
c. Act as Designated Accreditation/Approving Authority
d. Accredit information systems used to process classified information
e. Be accountable for actions on an IS (NISPOM 117.18)

13. International visit requests include the following examples EXCEPT:
a. One-time
b. Recurring

c. Initial (NISPOM 117.19)
d. Long-term
e. Emergency

14. Contractors shall deny cleared employee access to classified information when notified of:
a. Removal from JPAS, denial of clearance, revocation of clearance
b. Termination of employment, suspension or denial of clearance
c. Denial, revocation or suspension of clearance (NISPOM 117.10)
d. Removal from JPAS, adverse information, disclosure of classified information
e. Excessive drinking, debt, or unexplained affluence

15. The Tier 5 Investigation is required for:
a. SECRET, L, and CONFIDENTIAL PCLs
b. TOP SECRET, Q, and SCI access (DCSA Tier Investigations.pdf)
c. TOP SECRET only
d. SECRET only
e. All of the above

16. For an active DISS account status one must log in every _____ days.
a. 60
b. 90
c. 30
d. 45
e. 180

17. Which fields are required for looking up a person in DISS?
a. Last name
b. First and last name
c. Social Security Number and last name
d. First, middle and last name and Social Security Number
e. Social Security Number

18. For a Tier 5 investigation, you must provide work experience for the past _____ years.
a. 10
b. 20
c. 7
d. 5
e. 3

19. The FSO or designee shall review the SF 86 to determine:
a. Adequacy and accuracy
b. Completeness and accuracy
c. Adequacy and completeness (NISPOM 117.10)
d. Accuracy and timeliness
e. Completeness and timeliness

20. What level of classified information should be maintained under an information management system?
a. CONFIDENTIAL
b. SECRET
c. TOP SECRET
d. b and c
e. All of the above (NISPOM 117.15)

21. Where initial response teams consist of uncleared employees, which of the following response times apply?
a. 72 hours
b. 48 hours
c. A reasonable amount of time (NISPOM 117.15)
d. 30 days
e. 45 days

22. In which situations are contractors permitted to grant clearances?
a. If work begins within 30 days of granting FCL or PCL
b. Under supervision of CSA
c. Never (NISPOM 117.10)
d. If necessary for performance on contract
e. When directed by CSA

23. The SF 312 is an agreement between _____ and _____.
a. FSO, individual
b. FSO, CSA
c. United States, FSO
d. United states, cleared individual (NISPOM 117.8 and SF 312)
e. CSA, individual

24. Methods of approved refresher training include:
a. Briefings
b. Instructional materials
c. Videos
d. All of the above (NISPOM 117.12)
e. a and c

25. Export control regulation violations subjecting classified information to be compromised by foreign nationals shall be reported to:
a. GCA
b. Contractor
c. CSA (NISPOM 117.19)
d. State Department
e. DGR

26. The contractual guidance provided for performing on classified contracts is found in:
a. Security Guidance Form
b. Security Specification Guide

c. Contract Security Classification Specification (NISPOM 117.13)
d. Classified Work on Contracts Guidance
e. None of the above

27. Initially, who should the contractor notify in the event of challenge of classification?
a. CSA
b. CSO
c. GCA (NISPOM 117.13)
d. GSA
e. CUR

28. Freight forwarders who take custody of classified material must have:
a. FCL
b. Adequate space
c. Proper security level storage capacity
d. a and b
e. a and c (NISPOM 117.19)

29. What must the contractor do in cases of inadvertent release of classified material?
a. Determine clearance and access of holder
b. Provide written notice to those cleared for access of the proper classification
c. Determine if control of material has been lost
d. a and c
e. All of the above (NISPOM 117.8)

30. Contractors should _____ during implementation of inspection procedures and bring significant problems to the _____.
a. Seek legal advice, FSO
b. Consult KMPs, CSA
c. Consult CSA, FSO
d. Consult FSO, CSA
e. Seek legal advice, CSA (NISPOM 117.15)

31. Security reviews may not be conducted more than every _____ unless special circumstances exist.
a. 180 days
b. 26 weeks
c. 18 months
d. 24 months
e. None of the above-Depends on risk (NISPOM 117.15)

32. Which positions must be cleared to the same access level of the FSO and FCL?
a. Senior management official and Insider Threat Program Senior Official (NISPOM 117.7)
b. FSO and KMP's
c. CSO and senior management official CEO
d. ISSO and ISSM
e. KMP and ISSM

33. Reports of events impacting the FCL status should be submitted to:
a. FSO
b. GCA
c. CSA (NISPOM 117.8)
d. GSA
e. a and c

34. Alternative Compensatory Control Measures include items identified as:
a. SECRET
b. CONFIDENTIAL
c. SAP
d. TOP SECRET
e. None of the Above

35. How many days from the date access to cryptographic information is not needed must an employee be debriefed?
a. 30 days
b. 90 days (NISPOM 117.21)
c. 180 days
d. Two years
e. One year

36. Temporary PCLs apply to which of the following?
a. TOP SECRET
b. SECRET
c. CONFIDENTIAL
d. All of the above (NISPOM 117.10)
e. b and c

37. If a company falls under FOCI, who is responsible for deciding that a limited entity eligibility is appropriate?
a. FSO
b. CSO
c. FBI
d. CSA (NISPOM 117.11)
e. GCA

38. The NISP was established by:
a. Executive Order 12829 (NISPOM 117.1)
b. Executive Order 12333
c. Executive Order 13355
d. Executive Order 12356
e. Executive Order 12345

39. Written authorization of the _____ is required to transmit TOP SECRET information outside of the facility.
a. FSO
b. GCA (NISPOM 5-402)
c. CSA
d. CSO
e. DCSA

40. Who can approve transmission of CNWDI classified outside of the facility?
a. GCA (NISPOM 117.20)
b. CSA
c. FSO
d. CIA
e. FBI

41. Which of the following is true about information system passwords?
a. Protected in the same manner as information on the system
b. Protected at the same level as the information on the system
c. Changed in frequency to meet the level of risk assessed by CSA
d. a and c
e. All of the above (NISPOM 117.18)

42. Which of the following constitute a primary reason(s) to reproduce TOP SECRET documents?
a. As required by operational needs (32 CFR 2001.45)
b. When directed by FSO
c. When directed by CSA
d. Contract is renewed
e. All of the above

43. Who is responsible as designated to receive TOP SECRET information?
a. TASCO
b. SAPCO
c. TSCO (NISPOM 117.15)
d. ISSO
e. ITPSO

44. Concerning classified information, _____ must be destroyed as soon as practical after it has served its purpose.
a. Multiple copies (NISPOM 117.15)
b. Original documents
c. Classified waste
d. a and b
e. All of the above

45. Storing information in a _____ may be necessary when other normal means are unsuitable or impractical:
a. Supplemental protection
b. Closed area (NISPOM 117.15)
c. Open area
d. Restricted area
e. None of the above

46. For _____ material, only areas protected by IDS will qualify for open storage:
a. CONFIDENTIAL
b. TOP SECRET
c. SECRET (32 CFR 2001.43)
d. UNCLASSIFIED
e. a and c

47. When should TOP SECRET information be taken into accountability?
a. When transmitted outside of the facility (NISPOM 117.15)
b. Immediately if not a finished document
c. Within 30 days of creation
d. Within 90 days of creation
b. None of the above

48. NATO has the following levels of security classification EXCEPT:
a. COSMIC TOP SECRET
b. NATO SECRET
c. NATO CONFIDENTIAL
d. NATO RESTRICTED
e. NATO TOP SECRET (NISPOM 117.19)

49. What is the level of FCL a contractor facility must have to access NATO RESTRICTED?
a. TOP SECRET
b. SECRET
c. CONFIDENTIAL
d. RESTRICTED
e. None of the above (NISPOM 117.20)

50. The wall construction in closed areas primary purpose is:
a. Offer resistance
b. Severe weather shelter
c. Provide evidence of unauthorized access (32 CFR 2001.53)
d. Protect from bomb blasts
e. a and c

51. Central monitoring stations may be located at which UL-listed location:
a. Military Operations Center
b. Emergency Operations Center
c. Cleared residential monitoring station (NISPOM 117.15)

d. Uncleared commercial central station
e. All of the above

52. Central monitoring records shall be maintained indicating:
a. Time of the alarm
b. Names of security force detail responding
c. Time dispatched
d. Time of arrival
e. All of the above (NISPOM 117.15)

53. The NISPOM also provides guidance for the classes of classified information including:
a. Restricted Data, COMSEC, CONFIDENTIAL, Unrestricted Data
b. Restricted Data, Formerly Restricted Data, Sensitive Compartmented Information and Special Access Program (NISPOM 117.1)
c. COMSEC, Unrestricted Data, SECRET, Special Access Program
d. Restricted Data, CONFIDENTIAL, Sensitive Compartmented Information
e. Restricted Data, COMSEC, Sensitive Compartmented Information, Special Access Program

54. The Director Information Security Oversight Office, ______ and ______ the NISP implementation directive.
a. Measures and reads
b. Dictates and enforces
c. Issues and maintains (NISPOM 117.1)
d. Installs and supervises
e. Writes and enforces

55. The overall classification shall be marked on which part of the document:
a. Top and bottom of outside cover
b. Title page
c. First page
d. All of the above (ISOO booklet "Marking Classified National Security Information")
e. a and b

56. Which markings are appropriate for identifying the source of classification?
a. DERIVED FROM (NISPOM 117.13)
b. DECLASSIFY ON
c. WRITTEN BY
d. All of the above
e. a and b

57. What must contractors determine and establish while hosting classified visits:
a. Identification of visitors
b. Appropriate PCL
c. Duration of meeting
d. Type of media used
e. a and b (NISPOM 117.16)

58. Which of the following are part of "DoD Components"?
a. DOE
b. DOJ
c. FBI
d. CIA
e. Military Departments (NISPOM 117.2)

59. Which of the following are types of international visit request?
a. Initial
b. Follow-up
c. Amendment (NISPOM 117.19)
d. Special
e. Annual

60. If a contractor's FCL is terminated, how must classified documents be disposed of?
a. Return to GCA or as instructed by CSA (NISPOM 117.9)
b. Return to CSA
c. Return to winning contractor
d. Destroy unless declassified
e. Ask for retention until FCL is reinstated

61. Who would provide guidance for the destruction of classified material?
a. GCA
b. CSA (NISPOM 117.9)
c. FSO
d. GSA
e. CSO

62. Requests for government sponsored meetings should address all EXCEPT:
a. Dates of meeting
b. Location of meeting
c. Content of announcements
d. List of foreign representatives
e. Seating arrangements (NISPOM 117.16)

63. Need to know for meetings are determined by:
a. Holder of classified material
b. Contractor
c. Authorizing agency (NISPOM 117.16)
d. FSO
e. Visitor

64. For a classified contract, a _____ and a _____ shall be incorporated in the solicitations and subcontract.
a. Security requirements clause, Security Classification Guide
b. DD form 254, FCL
c. FCL, Security Classification Guide

d. Security requirements clause, Contract Security Classification Specification (NISPOM 117.17)
e. DD Form 254, Security Classification Guide

65. The _____ shall be notified if the CSA discovers unsatisfactory security conditions in a subcontractor facility.
a. GCA
b. GSA
c. Prime contractor (NISPOM 117.17)
d. Subcontractor
e. CSO

66. Which of the roles listed are responsibilities of the ISSM:
a. Accreditation/Approving Authority
b. Accredit information systems used to process classified information
c. Oversee development of facility IS Security Programs (NISPOM 117.18)
d. Conduct risk management procedures based on contractor's facility
e. None of the above

67. Which E.O. provides information on marking classified email?
a. E.O. 12353
b. E.O. 13526 (NISPOM 117.12)
c. E.O. 11257
d. E.O. 13691
e. E.O. 12563

68. Confidential material may be transmitted outside of the U.S. by which means?
a. Registered mail through U.S. Military postal facilities
b. Cleared contractor employees
c. Designated courier
d. Cleared commercial carrier
e. All of the above (32 CFR 2001.46)

69. TOP SECRET material shall be stored in:
a. GSA approved security container
b. Approved vault
c. Approved closed area with supplemental controls
d. a and c
e. All of the above (32 CFR 2001.43)

70. Under SEAD and CSA guidance, what should contractors report?
a. Provide general information about protection of classified information
b. Provide reports to CSA, FBI and ISOO as required (NISPOM 117.8)
c. Reports should be from the cleared employee to the CSA
d. When reports are classified, the Privacy Act does not apply to reports
e. All of the above

71. NSA is a government agency having classification jurisdiction over:
a. DOE
b. RD
c. COMSEC (117.11)
d. FRD
e. DNI

72. How often should an inventory of TOP SECRET information be conducted?
a. Bi-annually
b. Annually (NISPOM 117.15)
c. Semi-annually
d. Every 18 months
e. Every three years

73. Which level of classified information must follow a continuous receipt system?
a. CONFIDENTIAL
b. SECRET
c. TOP SECRET (NISPOM 117.15)
d. b and c
e. All of the above

74. Working papers shall be marked the same as finished documents and at the same classification level. Which answer is correct concerning retention?
a. Transmitted within the facility
b. Retained for more than 30 days from creation for TOP SECRET
c. Retained for more than 180 days from creation for SECRET (NISPOM 117.15)
d. Retained for more than 120 days from creation for SECRET
e. Retained for more than 120 days from creation for CONFIDENTIAL

75. The CSA can authorize up to _____ when factors preclude quicker alarm response time.
a. Thirty minutes (NISPOM 117.15)
b. Fifteen minutes
c. Twenty minutes
d. One hour
e. What is reasonable to safeguard classified material

76. Which of the following can the CSA approve when no other alarm response options are available?
a. Response by neighborhood watch
b. Monitor by hidden camera
c. Guarded by working dogs
d. Installation of wire security
e. Response by cleared employee (NISPOM 117.15)

77. Classified intelligence documents at a contractor facility shall be controlled according to NISPOM, with possible additional instructions from:
a. NRC
b. DNI

c. CSA
d. Intelligence Community Directives (NISPOM 117.23)
e. FSO

78. The minimum investigation requirement for Q, TOP SECRET, and SCI levels is:
a. Non-critical sensitive
b. Moderate risk
c. Critical sensitive (NISPOM 117.10)
d. Special risk
e. Polygraph

79. The minimum investigation requirement for SECRET is:
a. Non-critical sensitive (NISPOM 117.10)
b. Critical sensitive
c. Special sensitive
d. High risk
e. Polygraph

80. Only contractors with access to RD and FRD can be trained and designated as _____ .
a. FRD Classifiers
b. RD derivative classification authority (NISPOM 117.23)
c. NRC Classifiers
d. DOE Classifiers
e. DoD Classifiers

81. Cleared contractor employees must be briefed by the _____ prior to having access to CNWDI.
a. CSA
b. GCA
c. DOE
d. NRC
e. FSO (NISPOM 117.20)

82. Accountability records for COSMIC TOP SECRET ATOMAL must be maintained for:
a. 10 years (NISPOM 117.19
b. Two years
c. Five years
d. Three years
e. Four years

83. Recommendations for the downgrading of NATO classified information should be forwarded to:
a. Originating activity
b. CSA
c. GSA
d. CUSR (NISPOM 117.19)
e. FSCC

84. Under the insider threat plan, who is responsible to ensure that insider threat awareness is developed for IS users?
a. CSO
b. ISSO
c. FSO
d. FBI
e. ISSM (NISPOM 117.18)

85. All of the following require accountability receipts EXCEPT:
a. NATO SECRET
b. NATO SECRET ATOMAL
c. COSMIC TOP SECRET
d. NATO CONFIDENTIAL (NISPOM 117.19)
e. NATO CONFIDENTIAL ATOMAL

86. Which of the following characteristics is not used to describe a contractor?
a. Grantee
b. Certificate holder
c. Employee (NISPOM 117.3)
d. Licensee
e. None of the above

87. An approved vault is constructed according to guidance in the NISPOM and approved by the:
a. CSA (NISPOM 117.3)
b. GCA
c. FSO
d. ISSM
e. GSA

88. The structural integrity in closed areas should be ensured with:
a. Annual inspections
b. Monthly inspections
c. Contractor developed procedures (NISPOM 117.15)
d. Inspections every three months
e. Whenever directed by CSA

89. Prior to having access to COMSEC, _____ must have a final PCL at the appropriate level for the material of the account.
a. FSO
b. COMSEC account manager
c. Alternate COMSEC account manager
d. All of the above (NISPOM 117.21)
e. None of the above

90. When is it appropriate to mark an UNCLASSIFIED on classified documents and portions?
a. When document has been specifically reviewed to provide classification and those areas do not require classification (NISPOM 117.13)

b. When document is stored with classified information
c. When document contains FOUO information
d. When document is provided to GCA as a deliverable
e. All of the above

91. Disclosure authorizations may manifest by which of the following?
a. Export license
b. Technical assistance agreement
c. Letter of authorization or exemption to export requirements
d. Manufacturing license agreement
e. All of the above (NISPOM 117.19)

92. Which of the following is NOT required on a Visit Authorization Letter?
a. Contractors name
b. Level of PCL
c. Name of person to be visited
d. Contractors Social Security Number (NISPOM 117.16)
e. Contractors telephone number

93. International visit requests include the following examples EXCEPT:
a. One-time
b. Recurring
c. Initial (NISPOM 117.19)
d. Long-term
e. Emergency

94. The contractor should have approval of the _____ prior to requesting export authorization.
a. Contracts manager
b. GCA (NISPOM 117.19)
c. CSA
d. FSO
e. None of the above

95. TOP SECRET information can be transmitted outside of the U.S by which means?
a. DCS
b. Escort with Top Secret Clearance
c. Authorized Courier
d. a and c
e. All of the above (32 CFR 2001.46)

96. Which of the following apply to conducting inspections?
a. All persons entering or exiting are subject to search
b. Limit searches to buildings where classified work is performed
c. Perform inspections on a random basis
d. Not necessary where possible access to classified material is remote
e. All of the above (NISPOM 117.15)

97. Which are contractor inspection requirements required to reduce risk to classified information?
a. Perform inspections where unclassified work is performed
b. Perform inspections where classified work is performed (NISPOM 117.15)
c. Post notices of inspections where possibility of access is remote
d. a and c
e. All of the above

98. Which actions are contractors required to take while enforcing perimeter controls?
a. No less than annually
b. No less than every 6 months
c. 18 months from authorization
d. Every three years (NISPOM 117.18)
e. Only as required by GCA

99. May the CSA approve multiple stops while contract employee hand-carries classified material between countries?
a. Yes, if approved secure contractor storage is available
b. Never, only non-stop flights are authorized
c. Yes, if approved secure government storage is available (NISPOM 117.19)
d. Yes, as long as classified never leaves courier sight
e. None of the above

100. Which of the following are appropriate portion markings found on classified documents?
a. SECRET, TOP SECRET, CONFIDENTIAL
b. S, TS, C (Marking Classified National Security Information)
c. UNCLASSIFIED, TS, CONFIDENTIAL
d. FSO, TS, C, U
e. All of the above

101. Which change conditions are contractors required to report that may impact security clearance status?
a. Change of control of contractor
b. Change in contractor ownership
c. Significant stock transfers
d. a and c
e. All of the above (NISPOM 117.7)

102. Sometimes classified material is created while working on a classified project. In many cases it will be destroyed as soon as possible. How should this information developed be marked?
a. No marking required
b. With the highest level of information in the project (NISPOM 117.13)
c. MISCELLANEOUS CLASSIFIED
d. THIS INFORMATION IS MISCELLANEOUS
c. Nonc of thc abovc

103. It is the responsibility of _____ to indicate that information is "In Confidence".
a. CSA
b. Foreign government (NISPOM 117.19)
c. FSO
d. GCA
e. CSO

104. The _____ serves as Executive Agent for the NISP.
a. Secretary of State
b. Department of the Army
c. Secretary of Defense (NISPOM 117.7)
d. Department of Defense
e. Secretary of State

105. Which of the following is a requirement for closed area vault doors?
a. 8 inches thick
b. CSA approved
c. GCA approved
d. GSA approved (NISPOM 117.15)
e. 4 inches thick

106. Which organization acts as CSA for the DoD?
a. Secretary of Energy
b. Director DCSA
c. Under Secretary of Defense for Intelligence & Security (NISPOM 117.6)
d. Director of National Intelligence
e. Director of DOJ

107. Information is downgraded or declassified based on:
a. Political stabilization
b. Loss of sensitivity (NISPOM 117.13)
c. Verification of public disclosure
d. Loss of application
e. Expiration of contract

108. Where should classification markings NOT appear on a classified document?
a. Front cover
b. Back cover
c. Title
d. Illustrations and charts
e. Sentences in a paragraph (ISOO booklet "Marking Classified National Security Information")

109. Consultants can be cleared, however their performance on classified work is limited to:
a. The contractor facility unless in execution of authorized visits (NISPOM 117.10)
b. Consultant home office with approved FCL
c. Consultant home office with contractor escort
d. Discretion of DD Form 254
e. All of the above

110. Which of the following are exempt from classification markings because of difficulty in marking?
a. Files
b. Folders
c. Email
d. Microfiche
e. None of the above (ISOO booklet "Marking Classified National Security Information")

TEST 4 Answers-Long Version

1. When requesting the retention of CONFIDENTIAL material beyond two years, the contractor can identify it by approximate number of documents and _____.
a. General subject matter (NISPOM 117.15)
b. Author's name
c. Media type
d. Title
e. Date of creation

2. Pulverizing may only be used to destroy these kinds of products:
a. Paper (32 CFR 2001.47)
b. Metal
c. Plastic
d. Rubber
e. Computer

3. Which cleared employee, identified by position, ensures that insider threat awareness is developed for IS users?
a. CSA
b. GCA
c. FSO
d. ISSM (NISPOM 117.18)
e. FBI

4. The Director of National Intelligence prescribes the sections of NISPOM that address _____ and _____ including _____.
a. Operations, intelligence sources, procurement
b. Intelligence sources, methods, SCI (NISPOM 117.23)
c. SAP, intelligence sources, means
d. Organization, classification, procurement
e. Classification, dissemination, intelligence sources

5. The FSO shall complete training as considered appropriate by the:
a. CSA (NISPOM 117.12)
b. GCA
c. GSA
d. NISPOM Training Annex
e. Senior ranking officer

6. A contractor should cooperate with Government agencies during official investigations. Which is a more likely scenario this cooperation could be demonstrated through?
a. Providing suitable place to conduct interview (NISPOM 117.7)
b. Providing company car for offsite inspections
c. Providing computer access
d. a and b
e. All of the above

7. Which of the following determines a contractor's eligibility for access to classified information?
a. DISCO
b. Adjudication Agency
c. CSA (NISPOM 117.9)
d. FSO
e. All of the above

8. Critical Nuclear Weapon Design Information is a _____ category of SECRET Restricted Data or TOP SECRET Restricted Data.
a. DOE
b. DoD (NISPOM 117.12)
c. NRC
d. CSA
e. DOT

9. Employees sign certificates stating that they have been given a NATO security briefing. Certificates for NATO SECRET are maintained for:
a. Three years
b. Two years (NISPOM 117.19)
c. Five years
d. Six years
e. Four years

10. For international transfers of classified material, follow-up action is sent through CSA if a signed receipt is not returned within:
a. 30 days
b. 15 days
c. 45 days (NISPOM 117.19)
d. 3 days
e. 10 days

11. An emergency visit request is usually submitted within _____ calendar days of proposed visit.
a. 21
b. 4
c. 15
d. 7 (NISPOM 117.19)
e. 36

12. Which change conditions are contractors required to report that may impact security clearance status?
a. Change of control of contractor
b. Change in contractor ownership
c. Significant stock transfers
d. a and c
e. All of the above (NISPOM 117.7)

13. Which is a responsibility of the Secretary of Energy?
a. Authority for procedures for information classified under AEA
b. Authority over access to information classified under AEA
c. Authority over portions pertaining to information classified as RD
d. Authority over portions pertaining to information classified as FRD
e. All of the above (NISPOM 117.6)

14. All of the following should be documented on the SF 86 EXCEPT:
a. Deceased parents
b. Deceased father-in-law
c. Deceased mother-in-law
d. Deceased cousins
e. All should be reported

15. How long will the FSO maintain a copy of an employee's SF 86?
a. Five years
b. Ten years
c. Until clearance is granted or denied (NISPOM 117.10)
d. Until employee terminates employment
e. 180 days

16. Refresher security training for cleared employees must be completed at least:
a. Every six months
b. Annually (NISPOM 117.12)
c. Quarterly
d. Every three months
e. Upon discretion of FSO

17. Central monitoring stations shall be required to:
a. Monitor each alarmed area (NISPOM 117.15)
b. Have video surveillance
c. Have remote access to doors
d. Report hourly to guards
e. Call periodically during storms

18. Subcontracted guards must be under a classified contract with which of the following?
a. GCA, CSA
b. CSA, DCSA
c. Cleared contractor facility (NISPOM 117.15)
d. Monitoring station, installing alarm company
e. All of the above

19. Contractors who paraphrase classified information are making _____ decisions:
a. Reasons for classification
b. Security Classification Guidance
c. Derivative classification (NISPOM 117.3)
d. Classification
e. Classified document

20. A U.S. contractor's ability to access classified information stored abroad is the responsibility of:
a. GCA
b. U.S. Government (NISPOM 117.19)
c. CSA
d. State Department
e. DGR

21. U.S. RESTRICTED AND FORMERLY RESTRICTED Data is marked all EXCEPT:
a. COSMIC TOP SECRET ATOMAL
b. NATO RESTRICTED ATOMAL (NISPOM 117.19)
c. NATO CONFIDENTIAL ATOMAL
d. NATO SECRET ATOMAL
e. None of the above

22. Which entity is required to review and revise the Contract Security Classification Specification when change occurs?
a. CSO
b. GCA (NISPOM 117.13)
c. CSA
d. FSO
e. GSA

23. Which are appropriate page markings for a document classified at the SECRET level?
a. SECRET, TOP SECRET, SENSITIVE, CONFIDENTIAL
b. CONFIDENTIAL, SECRET, UNCLASSIFIED (NISPOM 117.13)
c. CONFIDENTIAL, FOUO, TOP SECRET
d. UNCLASSIFIED, FOUO, SENSITIVE
e. All of the above

24. During UNCLASSIFIED visits by foreign nationals, it is a _____ responsibility to ensure export authorizations are obtained.
a. GCA
b. Contractor (NISPOM 117.19)
c. CSA
d. State Department
e. DGR

25. Which organization acts as CSA for the DoD?
a. Secretary of Energy
b. Director DCSA

c. Under Secretary of Defense for Intelligence & Security (NISPOM 117.6)
d. Director of National Intelligence
e. Director of DOJ

26. Which of the following duties may a designated ISSO perform?
a. Certify that system security plan is implemented
b. Recommend self-inspection corrective actions (NISPOM 117.18)
c. Develop information system security programs
d. Command security resources
e. Grant IATOs

27. TOP SECRET control officials shall be designated to _____, _____, _____TOP SECRET information.
a. Transmit, maintain access and accountability records for, and receive (NISPOM 117.15)
b. Create, classify, brief, document
c. Receive, create, classify, disseminate
d. Request, assign, account, disseminate
e. Receive, transmit, classify, document

28. Classified working papers generated by contractors in preparation of finished project shall be:
a. Dated when created
b. Marked with overall classification and annotated "WORKING PAPERS"
c. Stored separately from finished documents
d. a and b (NISPOM 117.13)
e. All of the above

29. What frequency of security reviews shall be conducted on cleared facilities?
a. Periodic
b. CSA determines (NISPOM 117.7)
c. Annual
d. Semi-Annual
e. Monthly

30. Contractors are required to report:
a. Events that have an impact on FCLs
b. Events that have an impact on PCLs
c. Events that have an impact on ability to safeguard classified information
d. All of the above (NISPOM 117.8)
e. b and c

31. When should a contractor sign a receipt for transmission of CONFIDENTIAL material?
a. Not a requirement (NISPOM 117.15)
b. Always a requirement
c. If receipt has errors
d. a and c
e. All of the above

32. Information classified as SECRET can be transmitted outside of facility by all means EXCEPT:
a. Defense Courier Service, if authorized by GCA
b. U.S. Postal Service Registered Mail
c. U.S. Postal Service Priority Mail (32 CFR 2001.46)
d. Cleared commercial carrier
e. Cleared commercial messenger service

33. What should the FSO do with original, signed copies of the SF 86 and the Authorization for Release of Information and Records before access eligibility is granted or denied?
a. Send to GCA
b. Send to FBI
c. Retain (NISPOM 117.10)
d. Return to applicant
e. All of the above

34. Which of the following is NOT an insider threat training topic for all cleared personnel?
a. Detecting insider threats
b. Reporting insider threats
c. Applicable legal policies (NISPOM 117.12)
d. Counterintelligence reporting requirements
e. Threat behavior indicators

35. All the following provide an appropriate proof of U.S. citizenship EXCEPT:
a. Driver's license (NISPOM 117.10)
b. Birth Certificate
c. Expired Passport
d. DD Form 1966
e. Current Passport

36. Announcements of meetings shall be _____ and require government approval.
a. FOUO
b. SECRET
c. CONFIDENTIAL
d. UNCLASSIFIED (NISPOM 117.16)
e. TOP SECRET

37. Which of the following is NOT true concerning classified information in meetings?
a. Can be presented orally
b. Can be presented visually
c. Can be distributed to attendees (NISPOM 117.16)
d. Attendees must turn in classified notes
e. Classified notes will be disseminated per NISPOM

38. When wrapping classified material for shipment, the _____ cannot go on the outer label:
a. Classification level (32 CFR 2001.46)
b. Office code letter
c. Office code number

d. Directions for routing
e. Facility name

39. All of the following must be included in the authorization letter for hand carrying classified material on a commercial aircraft EXCEPT:
a. Traveler's Social Security Number (32 CFR 2001.46)
b. Description of traveler's ID
c. Description of material being carried
d. Identify points of departure, destination, and known transfer point
e. Location and telephone number of CSA

40. Contractors shall limit the number of PCL requests to:
a. One third of the company
b. KMPs and direct reports
c. That which is necessary to operate efficiently (NISPOM 117.9)
d. Meet future requirements for classified contracts
e. That which is specifically outlined on the DD Form 254

41. The NISP applies to which agency(s)?
a. NRC
b. CIA
c. NRA
d. Secretary of Defense (NISPOM 117.2)
e. NSC

42. Among other requirements, the destruction records for TOP SECRET must contain the _____ and be kept for _____.
a. Date of destruction, two years (NISPOM 117.15)
b. SSN of destroyer, two years
c. Name of destroyer, one year
d. ID material destroyed, one year
e. Date of Classification, five years

43. Which is not a training requirement for the Insider Threat Program personnel as described in NISPOM?
a. Security Fundamentals
b. Insider threat response procedures
c. Safety considerations (NISPOM 117.12)
d. Privacy Policies
e. Consequences of misusing collected records and data

44. Which types of door locking devices are approved protecting stored SECRET and CONFIDENTIAL information?

a. Key operated lock (32 CFR 2001.43)
b. Hand print reader
c. Deadbolt lock
d. Swipe card reader
e. All of the above

45. Which E.O. provides guidance for safeguarding USG classified information?

a. E.O. 12353
b. E.O. 12829 (NISPOM 117.1)
c. E.O. 11257
d. E.O. 13691
e. E.O. 12563

46. Which E.O. provides information on marking classified email?

a. E.O. 12353
b. E.O. 13526 (NISPOM 117.12)
c. E.O. 11257
d. E.O. 13691
e. E.O. 12563

47. Which response force could the CSA approve as a last resort?

a. Cleared contractor employees (NISPOM 117.15)
b. Subcontracted guard force
c. Military police
d. Civil police
e. Proprietary security force

48. Need to know is generally based on:

a. Level of clearance
b. Block 13 of DD Form 254
c. Security Classification Guide
d. Contractual relationship (NISPOM 117.16)
e. As determined by CSA

49. Who has security oversight of contract employees who are long term visitors at government installations?

a. GCA
b. CSA
c. Contractor (NISPOM 117.16)
d. Host installation
e. CSO

50. 23. Which of the following are part of "DoD Components"?

a. DOE
b. DOJ

c. FBI
d. CIA
e. Military departments (NISPOM 117.2)

51. Which of the following characteristics is not used to describe a contractor?
a. Grantee
b. Certificate holder
c. Licensee
d. Employee (NISPOM 117.3)
e. None of the above

52. The NISP was established by:
a. Executive Order 12829 (NISPOM 117.1)
b. Executive Order 12333
c. Executive Order 13355
d. Executive Order 12356
e. Executive Order 12345

53. CONFIDENTIAL material may be stored the same as higher classification levels EXCEPT:
a. Supplemental controls are not necessary (32 CFR 2001.43)
b. Storage in steel filing cabinets do not apply to the October 1 2012 requirement
c. Storage cabinets do not have to be GSA approved
d. None of the above
e. All of the above

54. All of the following shall be transferred internationally through the CUSR Registry EXCEPT:
a. NATO SECRET
b. NATO SECRET ATOMAL
c. COSMIT TOP SECRET
d. NATO CONFIDENTIAL (NISPOM 117.19)
e. NATO CONFIDENTIAL ATOMAL

55. Which of the following are appropriate portion markings found on classified documents?
a. SECRET, TOP SECRET, CONFIDENTIAL
b. S, TS, C (Marking Classified National Security Information)
c. UNCLASSIFIED, TS, CONFIDENTIAL
d. FSO, TS, C, U
e. All of the above

56. Consultants can be cleared, however their performance on classified work is limited to:
a. The contractor facility unless in execution of authorized visits (NISPOM 117.10)
b. Consultant home office with approved FCL
c. Consultant home office with contractor escort
d. Discretion of DD Form 254
e. All of the above

57. Contractors shall submit reports to the:
a. FSO and DIA
b. FBI and CSA (NISPOM 117.8)
c. CSO and DIA
d. FBI and CIA
e. CIA and DIA

58. The government approves _____ before contractors can conduct a classified meeting at a contractor facility?
a. Attendees
b. Announcements
c. Security arrangements
d. All of the above (NISPOM 117.16)
e. None of the above

59. What actions must CSA take if FCL cannot be granted in sufficient time to qualify subcontractor for participating in current procurement actions?
a. Immediately cease processing
b. Continue processing for 90 days
c. Continue processing for 120 days
d. Continue processing (NISPOM 117.17)
e. None of the above

60. A contractor is any educational, industrial, commercial or any other entity that has been granted a(n) _____ by the _____.
a. PCL, GSA
b. FCL, GCA
c. FCL, CSA (NISPOM 117.3)
d. PCL, CSA
e. FCL, FSO

61. The _____ determines the duties of the ISSO:
a. CSA
b. GCA
c. FSO
d. ISSM (NISPOM 117.18)
e. FBI

62. Selection of appropriate protection measures should be based on:
a. Reaccreditation
b. System implementation
c. Re-evaluation of accreditation
d. Assessment of risk and conditions (NISPOM 117.18)
c. Annual rcvicw

63. If retention of classified documents under an expired contract is desired for longer than the 2-year period, who is the approval authority?
a. GCA (NISPOM 117.15)
b. CSA
c. FSO
d. FBI
e. CSO

64. What is the primary disposition of classified documents where retention has not been authorized?
a. Disseminate to winning bid contractor
b. Destroy unless declassified (NISPOM 117.15)
c. Maintain on site
d. a and c
e. None of the above

65. Need to know is generally based on:
a. Level of clearance
b. Block 13 of DD Form 254
c. Security Classification Guide
d. Contractual relationship (NISPOM 117.16)
e. As determined by CSA

66. Who receives reports of duplicate audits?
a. CSA
b. ISSM
c. FSO
d. GCA
e. ISOO (NISPOM 117.6)

67. TOP SECRET material shall be stored in:
a. GSA approved security container
b. Approved vault
c. Approved closed area with supplemental controls
d. a and c
e. All of the above (32 CFR 2001.43)

68. CSA approval to extend alarm response time may be annotated in the:
a. Standard Security Procedures
b. Alarm certificate
c. Monitoring station
d. Alarm System Description Form (NISPOM 117.15)
e. Guard check list

69. In the normal course of business contractors may disclose classified material to cleared individuals in all cases EXCEPT:
a. Company employees
b. MFO
c. Subcontractors
d. DoD activities
e. Between Federal Agencies (NISPOM 117.15)

70. When can authorized contractors disclose classified information to federal or state courts?
a. When instructed by the agency having jurisdiction over the information
b. When instructed by the attorney representing the U.S.
c. When instructed by the GCA
d. a and b (NISPOM 117.15)
e. All of the above

71. When downgrading or declassifying notification is contrary to markings shown, the contractor will remark to identify change and include:
a. Identify authority, date of action, identity of approving CSA
b. Date of action, identity of authority, position of person taking action (NISPOM 117.14)
c. Identity of authority, date of notification, identity of approving CSA
d. Identity of authority, date of notification, identity of contractor taking action
e. None of the above

72. What are the required elements of a derivatively classified document?
a. "DECLASSIFY ON"
b. "CLASSIFIED BY"
c. "DERIVED FROM"
d. None of the above
e. All of the above (ISOO Marking Classified National Security Information Booklet)

73. Open bin storage is not allowed for:
a. TOP SECRET (32 CFR 2001.43)
b. SECRET
c. CONFIDENTIAL
d. UNCLASSIFIED
e. a and b

74. The contractor shall document IS protection procedures in the _____.
a. SSP (NISPOM 117.18)
b. IS Certification Report
c. Master SPP
d. SPP
e. Security Classification Guide

75. Three types of investigations and reports contractors should send to the CSA include:
a. Initial, secondary and final
b. Preliminary, initial and final (NISPOM 117.8)

c. Initial, follow-up and final
d. Preliminary, initial and follow-up
e. Annual, refresher and final

76. What are some actions that a company may take during the FCL process?
a. Provide list of employees, submit SF 86 applications, process KMPs for PCLs
b. Execute CSA forms, process KMPs for PCLs, appoint U.S. citizen as FSO (NISPOM 117.7)
c. Execute CSA forms, submit SF 86 applications, provide list of employees
d. Provide list of employees, process KMPs for PCLs, appoint U.S. citizen as FSO
e. Provide list of employees, submit SF 86 applications, process KMPs for PCLs

77. All of the following require accountability receipts EXCEPT:
a. NATO SECRET
b. NATO SECRET ATOMAL
c. COSMIC TOP SECRET
d. NATO CONFIDENTIAL (NISPOM 117.19)
e. NATO CONFIDENTIAL ATOMAL

78. The only time RD and FRD shall be disclosed to international governments is:
a. When the US contractor and foreign government have an agreement
b. When the CSA and contractor have an agreement
c. When the United States and participating governments sign an agreement (NISPOM 117.23)
d. When the United States and all entities bid on information
e. When the US contractor and all entities sign treaty

79. The investigative tier standards for CONFIDENTIAL clearance investigations include:
a. Moderate risk (NISPOM 117.10)
b. High risk
c. Special Sensitive
d. Critical Sensitive
e. Polygraph

80. Which agencies determine which classified information to remove from the RD category to make it FRD?
a. DOE and DoD (NISPOM 117.3)
b. DOE and NRC
c. DoD and NRC
d. DoD and CSA
e. CSA and NRC

81. COSMIC TOP SECRET documents shall have reference numbers on:
a. Each page of the document (NISPOM 117.19)
b. The front and back covers
c. On the first page
d. On the title and first pages
e. On the appendix page

82. DTIC is responsible for remarking classification levels of documents after downgrading or declassification. The remarking occurs on all the following EXCEPT the:
a. Complete document (NISPOM 11-204)
b. Front and back covers
c. Title page
d. First page
e. Back pages

83. Where should classification information NOT appear on a classified document?
a. Each page
b. Each paragraph
c. Title (ISOO Marking Classified National Security Information)
d. Illustrations and charts
e. All of the above

84. In order to protect fragile intelligence resources and methods, _____ is responsible for parts of NISPOM that address SCI.
a. NSA
b. GCA
c. DNI (NISPOM 117.3)
d. CSA
e. GSA

85. Temporary TOP SECRET FCLs or PCLs are valid for access to COMSEC at the ____ and ____ levels.
a. SECRET, TOP SECRET
b. TOP SECRET, CONFIDENTIAL
c. CONFIDENTIAL, FOUO
d. SECRET, FOUO
e. CONFIDENTIAL, SECRET (NISPOM 117.10)

86. The COR establishes the COMSEC account and notifies the:
a. CSA (NISPOM 117.21)
b. GCA
c. FSO
d. NSA
e. DIA

87. Contractors maintain TOP SECRET reproduction records for _____ years.
a. Two years (NISPOM 117.15)
b. One year
c. Five years
d. Ten years
e. None of the above

88. Contractors are authorized to retain classified material received under contract for a period of _____ after completion of contract.
a. One year
b. Two years (NISPOM 117.13)
c. Five years
d. 180 days
e. 90 days

90. Which of the following is NOT true of the General Security Agreement between countries?
a. Limits use each governments information
b. Restricts third party transfers
c. Does not commit governments to share classified
d. Constitutes authority to release classified material to government (NISPOM 117.19)
e. Satisfies the eligibility requirements for foreign governments to protect U.S. classified defense articles

91. The _____ has oversight of contract security requirements on behalf of foreign governments.
a. CSA (NISPOM 117.19)
b. GCA
c. FSO
d. Contract manager
e. Embassy

92. All U.S. classified information must be transferred to the recipient government through its:
a. DGR (NISPOM 117.19)
b. GCA
c. COR
d. CSA
e. FSO

93. Which of the following types of carriers does NOT meet requirements for international transfer of classified material?
a. Chartered or owned by a NATO country (NISPOM 117.19)
b. Chartered or owned by recipient country
c. Chartered by the U.S.
d. Under U.S. Registry
e. Authorized by DSA of the GCA and security authorities of involved governments

94. The highest level of classified information that can be hand carried outside the U.S. is:
a. CONFIDENTIAL
b. FOUO
c. SECRET (NISPOM 117.19)
d. TOPSECRET
e. RESTRICTED

95. A U.S. company is under FOCI when:
a. A foreign interest creates job announcements in the U.S.
b. A foreign interest exercises power that may result in unauthorized disclosure of classified information (NISPOM 117.11)
c. A U.S. company markets product oversees
d. A foreign interests visit cleared facilities
e. A foreign involvement causes stock prices to fall

96. According to the Certificate Pertaining to Foreign Interests (SF 328), indicators that require reporting to the CSA include:
a. Organization owns 10% or more of total revenue or net income from any single foreign person
b. Five percent or more of voting securities held in shares that do not identify the beneficial owner
c. Organization owns 10 percent or more of any foreign interest (SF 328)
d. Organization has three or more contracts with a foreign person
e. KMPs make frequent visits to foreign countries

97. The dispatching company security officer must provide the receiving security officer with _____ advance notice of the couriers expected date and time of arrival.
a. 48 hours
b. 72 hours
c. 24 work hours (NISPOM 117.19)
d. 12 hours
e. 86 hours

98. All of the following are portion markings that one might find on foreign classified information EXCEPT:
a. TOP SECRET
b. SECRET
c. REGISTERED (NISPOM 117.14)
d. RESTRICTED or In Confidence
e. UNCLASSIFIED

99. Which of the following are considered a CSA?
a. Department of Defense
b. Central Intelligence Agency
c. Department of Energy
d. The Nuclear Regulatory Commission
e. All of the above (NISPOM 117.3)

100. Reference numbers on US originated NATO documents must be on _____ of a document:
a. Each page of the document
b. The front and back covers
c. The first page (NISPOM 117.19)
d. The title and first pages
e. The appendix page

101. Which of the following actions are required before a prime contractor can release information to a subcontractor?
a. Determine security requirements of the contract (NISPOM 117.17)
b. Ensure subcontractor has sufficient employees to safeguard classified information
c. Grant subcontractor necessary clearance
d. Evaluate closed area construction
e. Develop subcontractor access control requirements

102. What method of justification should a contractor submit to attend a classified meeting?
a. Provide information on the classified contract involved (NISPOM 117.16)
b. Cite the clearance level
c. Give company CAGE code
d. Submit job position
e. List qualifications

103. What should contractors ensure their derivative classifiers accomplish?
a. Be an original classifier
b. Complete derivative classifier training (NISPOM 117.12)
c. Complete a waiver if derivative classifier training is not available
d. Complete FSO certification training
e. a and c

104. The NISPOM also applies to classified information not released under a license, _____, grant, or certificate.
a. TAA
b. Contract (NISPOM 117.2)
c. License
d. Scope
e. Registration

105. Executive Order 12829 requires heads of agencies to enter into agreement with:
a. FSO
b. Foreign governments
c. Secretary of Defense (NISPOM 117.6)
d. Department of Labor
e. Department of Energy

106. How might a cleared contractor mark unclassified training material to simulate SECRET?
a. UNCLASSIFIED SAMPLE
b. SECRET FOR TRAINING PURPOSES
c. SECRET FOR TRAINING ONLY
d. SECRET FOR TRAINING, OTHERWISE UNCLASSIFIED (NISPOM 117.14)
e. All of the above

107. Which is not a training requirement for the Insider Threat Program Senior Official as described in NISPOM?
a. Counterintelligence Fundamentals
b. ITAR Fundamentals (NISPOM 117.12)
c. Security Fundamentals
d. Insider threat response procedures
e. Civil liberties policies

108. Initial Security Briefings should include which of the following?
a. Counterintelligence awareness
b. Cybersecurity awareness
c. Insider threat awareness
d. a and c
e. All of the above (NISPOM 117.12)

109. Derivative classifiers should be identified on derivatively classified documents by which means?
a. Name
b. Position
c. Identifier
d. a and b
e. All of the above (NISPOM 117.13)

110. _____ Security Agreements are negotiated with various foreign governments.
a. Multi-force
b. Bi-lateral (NISPOM 117.19)
c. Uni-lateral
d. Multi-lateral
e. Bi-layered

1. b
2. a
3. b
4. a
5. c
6. a
7. c
8. b
9. b
10. e
11. c
12. a
13. c
14. c
15. b
16. c
17. a
18. c
19. b
20. a
21. c
22. e
23. c
24. a
25. e
26. b
27. b
28. b
29. a
30. e
31. d
32. e
33. a
34. a
35. b
36. a
37. a
38. c
39. e
40. d
41. b
42. c
43. c
44. b
45. b
46. a
47. e
48. c
49. c
50. c
51. c
52. c
53. a
54. b
55. a
56. c
57. b
58. c
59. d
60. e
61. a
62. d
63. d
64. a
65. e
66. e
67. b
68. b
69. c
70. d
71. e
72. c
73. e
74. c
75. c
76. e
77. e
78. d
79. a
80. b
81. e
82. e
83. a
84. e
85. e
86. a
87. d
88. b
89. b
90. c
91. c
92. c
93. a
94. a
95. b
96. c
97. e
98. b
99. a
100. b
101. e
102. d
103. a
104. c
105. b
106. e
107. b
108. a
109. c
110. b

1. a
2. e
3. e
4. c
5. a
6. e
7. a
8. d
9. c
10. c
11. d
12. b
13. b
14. b
15. a
16. c
17. d
18. b
19. a
20. d
21. d
22. b
23. e
24. d
25. d
26. a
27. c
28. a
29. e
30. e
31. e
32. a
33. b
34. e
35. d
36. d
37. d
38. e
39. e
40. b
41. d
42. e
43. a
44. b
45. c
46. e
47. b
48. e
49. c
50. e
51. e
52. d
53. c
54. e
55. a
56. d
57. c
58. c
59. c
60. d
61. a
62. a
63. c
64. b
65. b
66. b
67. a
68. e
69. a
70. e
71. e
72. a
73. d
74. c
75. a
76. a
77. d
78. a
79. c
80. a
81. b
82. c
83. d
84. c
85. e
86. b
87. e
88. e
89. c
90. b
91. a
92. e
93. c
94. b
95. c
96. b
97. b
98. b
99. d
100. e
101. d
102. c
103. e
104. a
105. a
106. b
107. c
108. c
109. e
110. a

1. e
2. a
3. a
4. a
5. b
6. e
7. c
8. e
9. e
10. a
11. c
12. e
13. c
14. c
15. b
16. c
17. e
18. d
19. c
20. e
21. c
22. c
23. d
24. d
25. c
26. c
27. c
28. e
29. e
30. e
31. e
32. a
33. c
34. c
35. b
36. d
37. d
38. a
39. b
40. a
41. e
42. a
43. c
44. a
45. b
46. c
47. a
48. e
49. e
50. c
51. c
52. e
53. b
54. c
55. d
56. a
57. e
58. e
59. c
60. a
61. b
62. e
63. c
64. c
65. c
66. c
67. b
68. e
69. e
70. b
71. c
72. b
73. c
74. c
75. a
76. e
77. d
78. c
79. a
80. b
81. e
82. a
83. d
84. e
85. d
86. c
87. a
88. c
89. d
90. a
91. e
92. d
93. c
94. b
95. e
96. c
97. b
98. d
99. c
100. b
101. e
102. b
103. b
104. c
105. d
106. c
107. b
108. e
109. a
110. e

1. a
2. a
3. d
4. b
5. a
6. a
7. c
8. b
9. b
10. c
11. d
12. e
13. e
14. d
15. c
16. b
17. a
18. c
19. c
20. b
21. b
22. b
23. b
24. b
25. c
26. b
27. a
28. d
29. b
30. d
31. a
32. c
33. c
34. c
35. a
36. d
37. c
38. a
39. a
40. c
41. d
42. a
43. c
44. a
45. b
46. b
47. a
48. d
49. c
50. e
51. d
52. a
53. a
54. d
55. b
56. a
57. b
58. d
59. d
60. c
61. d
62. d
63. a
64. d
65. d
66. e
67. e
68. d
69. e
70. d
71. b
72. e
73. a
74. a
75. b
76. c
77. d
78. c
79. a
80. a
81. a
82. a
83. c
84. c
85. e
86. a
87. a
88. b
89. e
90. d
91. a
92. a
93. a
94. c
95. b
96. c
97. c
98. c
99. e
100. c
101. a
102. a
103. b
104. b
105. c
106. d
107. b
108. e
109. e
110. b

WHAT NEXT?

Perhaps at this time you are re-reading this chapter having become certified. You may be wondering what to do next. There is certainly more work to do as industrial security requirements continue to evolve. Current events have demonstrated this need for change as the security manager implements anti-terrorism into the threat matrix. I would recommend that you continue to engage with training, teaching, studying and growing. This will be necessary in maintaining your certifications. I encourage you to continue to improve your grasp of not only protecting our nation's assets, but protecting your employees and your product.

An industrial security professional may understand the process of requesting clearance actions, filing security paperwork, accounting for classified materials, building closed areas and performing per the Contract Security Classification Specification, DD Form 254. However, an industrial security manager should also understand physical security, prevention of workplace violence, risk analysis and security surveys, business continuity and physical security and IT convergence.

The security professional has other non-DoD resources available to improve their comprehension of the total job description. There are other certifications including the Certified Protection Professional (CPP) from ASIS International. Additional certifications and the study to earn those certifications increase the security professional's understanding of security. Along the way, they will learn tools to address security issues with corporate executives, present return on investment of security expenditures and create metrics for security effectiveness.

Thank you for continuing to develop your skills as an industrial security professional. We would also like to thank you for all you do to protect our way of life and guard our Nation's secrets. Our desire is that this book has encouraged your professional growth. If you have enjoyed this book, please feel free to leave a review as we want to hear your comments. Feel free to contact me using my website: www.redbikepublishing.com. I would also invite you to continue your studies with my books, *How to Get U.S. Government Contracts and Classified Work* and *Insider's Guide to Security Clearances*, as they make the perfect study companions. Also, consider browsing our other books before your next job interview; it will help increase your knowledge and awareness of security requirements and skills. We also invite you to download and study our NISPOM training. You can find training and other resources at www.redbikepublishing.com and www.bennettinstitute.com.

APPENDIX A-ESSAY QUESTIONS

These essay questions designed for those taking the ISOC certification exam. However, they can be applied toward ISP® certification as well. I recommend that all readers take the 110 question multiple choice exams first and then supplement with these essay style questions.

In this section, I have provided questions from the Industrial Security Oversight Certification (ISOC) Competency Preparatory Tools (CPTs) and the NISPOM paragraphs that provide answers. Take time to practice formulating the answers. You can answer in the book, but I recommend using your own paper to write out answers. The *Self-Inspection Handbook for NISP Contractors* also provides great study questions.

While studying this section, keep the following in mind:

- The earlier questions are from the point of view of contractors performing the tasks
- These questions are from the point of view of a government agency auditing the contractor performing the tasks
- The body of material covered on the ISP® and ISOC assessments cannot be memorized in its entirety. Use memory techniques only to help recall key points
- Focus on the application of accepted principles, practices, and theories, not memorizing facts, dates, and names

Practice Questions By Topic

Facility Clearance Requirements and Procedures

How would you explain the roles of facility clearance requirements and procedures in performing of industrial security oversight functions? (NISPOM 2-103, 2-104, 2-105, 2-107, 2-110 and 2-309)

What are the facility security clearance (FCL) requirements, including reporting requirements for changed conditions and organizational roles in processing new FCLs and changed conditions? (NISPOM 2-103, 2-104, 2-105, 2-107, 2-110 and 2-309)

Personnel Clearance Requirements and Procedures

How would you apply the criteria and requirements for accessing classified material (i.e., clearance, briefings, need- to-know)? (NISPOM 5-306, 5-313j, 5-314e, 6-601, 6-602)

What are eligibility requirements, eligibility limitations related to interim clearance, and eligibility determinations (e.g., revocations, denials, loss of jurisdiction, suspension, interim declinations)? (NISPOM 2-107, 2-211)

What are the background investigation and continuous evaluation standards and requirements? NISPOM 2-200e, 2-201, 2-204)

Business Structures

How would you recognize common business structures and discuss their industrial security oversight implications? (NISPOM 2-100 - 2-111)

How would you identify and explain common business structures (i.e., multiple facility organization (MFO), division, parent, subsidiary, home office (HOF)? (NISPOM 2-108 and 2-109)

What are the implications of business structures on facility clearance requirements and processes (i.e. Key Management Personnel (KMP) requirements, clearance/exclusion requirements, impact of KMP, corporate structure, ownership changes)? (NISPOM 2-102-2-106)

Counterintelligence (CI) Integration

How would you educate a contractor on CI threats/ vulnerabilities, potential mitigation strategies, and discuss their industrial security oversight implications? (NISPOM Chapter 3)

What methods do foreign nationals use to obtain information (e.g., social engineering, unsolicited emails, unsolicited requests, elicitation, recruitment, cyber threats)? (NISPOM 3-107)

What are the foreign collection and reporting requirements? (NISPOM 1-208, 3-107, 2-302)

Foreign Ownership, Control or Influence (FOCI) Fundamentals

What are FOCI terms, factors, and actions in National Industrial Security System? (NISPOM 1-302g, 2-102, 2-300, 2-301-2-309)

What are the roles of outside directors, proxy holders, voting trustees, and members of the Government Security Committee? (NISPOM 2-305-2-308)

What are the purpose of FOCI oversight, agreement compliance, and annual FOCI compliance meetings? (NISPOM 2-308)

International Security Requirements

How would you apply international security requirements in performing industrial security oversight functions? (NISPOM Chapter 10)

What are the basic requirements for the international transfer of classified information (i.e., government-to- government transfers), and the roles/ responsibilities of the Designated Government Representative (DGR)? (NISPOM 10-400-10-408)

What are the purpose of transportation plans, security communications, and hand-carries (all methods of international transfers)? (NISPOM 10-401, 10-402, 10-405)

What is the purpose of Technology Plans in regards to processing and controlling of Foreign Visitors? (NISPOM 10-507, 10-510)

Information Systems Security

What are the fundamentals of information systems security in performing industrial security oversight functions? (NISPOM Chapter 8)

List and define the basic information system security terminology:

- system security plan (SSP) (NISPOM 8-102)
- information system security manager (ISSM) (NISPOM 8-103)
- risk management framework (RMF) (National Institute of Standards and Technology Special Publication 800-37, "Guide for Applying the Risk Management Framework to Federal Information Systems: A Security Life Cycle Approach" February 2010, as amended http: //csrc.nist.gov/publications/)

- interim action to operate/action to operate (IATO/ATO) (NISPOM 8-202)

Specialized Mission Areas

What is your role in supporting each of the following in performing industrial security oversight functions?

- Communications Security (COMSEC) (NISPOM 9-400-9-408)

- Special Access Programs (SAPs) (NISPOM Appendix D)

Specialized Briefings/ Education

How would you administer special briefings? (NISPOM 3-100-3-109) As you read, be prepared to answer:

- How would you verify the completion and effectiveness of security education at contractor facilities?

- How would you discuss their industrial security oversight implications?

What are the initial briefing administrative, content, and documentation requirements? (NISPOM 3-107)

How would you explain refresher briefing administrative requirements? (NISPOM 3-108)

Contractor/ Sub-Contractor Reporting Responsibilities

How would you discuss the rationale underlying contractor/sub-contractor reporting requirements? NISPOM 5-502, NISPOM Chapter 7)

What are the requirements for reporting actual, probable, or possible espionage, sabotage, or subversive activities? (NISPOM 1-300 - 1-304)

What are the requirements for reporting suspicious contact? (NISPOM 1-302)

What are the requirements for reporting an insider threat? (NISPOM 1-300, 3-103)

What are the requirements for reporting routine changes in cleared employee status, such as marriage, divorce, termination, or death of employee? (NISPOM 1-302)

What are the requirements for reporting on foreign classified contracts? (NISPOM 10-201, 10-301, 10-510, 10-718)

Classification and Retention

How would you validate the implementation of classification and retention requirements in performing industrial security oversight functions? (NISPOM 5-700-5-708)

What are the purpose, elements, use, and process for the issuance of DD Form 254? (NISPOM 7-101 and 7-102)

What is the role of prime contractors with respect to security requirements for sub-contractors? (NISPOM 7-101 and 7-102)

What are requirements and limitations for retention authorities (e.g., automatic retention period, DD Form 254, bid proposal, final DD Form 254)? (NISPOM 5-701, 7-103)

What is the industry role and responsibility with respect to derivative classification (including training requirements)? (NISPOM 4-102)

Safeguard/ Storage and Classified Material Controls

How would you validate the implementation of protection measures for safeguarding and storing classified material in performing industrial security oversight functions? (NISPOM Chapter 5)

What are the storage requirements for materials at various classifications? (NISPOM 5-300-5-314)

What are the physical controls associated with classified information system processing? (NISPOM 5-300-5-314, 8-302)

What are the end-of-day security requirements? (NISPOM 5-102)

What are the processes for restricted area identification and physical and procedural requirements? (NISPOM 5-305)

What are the supplemental controls (e.g., intrusion detection system, grandfathered guards, security in-depth) for closed areas? (NISPOM 5-306)

Classified Visits and Meetings

What are the security requirements and procedures for classified meetings and visits in performing industrial security oversight functions? (NISPOM 6-100-6-203)

What are the different classified visit determinations, request elements, transmittal methods, and procedures? (NISPOM 6-100-6-203)

What are the facility visitor control procedures (e.g., need-to-know determinations, visit authorizations, long-term visitor specifications, expert technology control plan (TCP))? (NISPOM 6-100-6-104, 10-508-10-509)

Security Review Procedures

Another great resource, other than NISPOM references here, is the *Self-Inspection Handbook for NISP Contractors* available to download from www.dcsa.mil and print version from www.redbikepublishing.com. This handbook is a topical self assessment that will familiarize test takers with the type of oversight questions that can be helpful for ISOC study.

How would you conduct security reviews under NISP, and identify and substantiate security review findings in performing industrial security oversight functions? (NISPOM 1-207)

What are the security review process, guidelines, and guidance? NISPOM 1-207, www.dcsa.com, *Self-Inspection Handbook for NISP Contractors*

What are the security training and briefing standards (e.g., inclusion of CI, reproduction, derivative classification, and disposition)? (NISPOM Chapter 3-100-3-109)

Security Violations and Administrative Inquiry Procedures

How would you evaluate security incident and violation reports for completeness and conduct administrative inquiries in performing industrial security oversight functions? (NISPOM 1-303, 1-400-1-402, 8-101, 8-302)

What are the facility security officer (FSO) and ISSM responsibilities pertaining to security violations? (NISPOM 1-203, 1-303, 1-400-1-402, 8-101, 8-302)

What are the definitions for loss, compromise, and suspected compromise of classified information?

Notes

Notes

CONCLUSION

This concludes our book and I hope you have found it informative and useful. I also hope that I have delivered on my promise of helping you prepare to take the ISP® and ISOC exams.

ABOUT THE AUTHOR

Jeffrey W. Bennett, ISOC, ISP®, SAPPC, SFPC is a security expert with experience in the Army, U.S. Government and as a Facility Security Officer (FSO). Jeff is enthusiastic about protecting our nation's secrets. He believes that integrity, influence and credibility are paramount qualities required of security professionals. His primary goal is to show Cleared Defense Contractors how to bring about security awareness, build influence within the organization and to make a difference where they work.

He speaks, writes, consults and provides products to help professionals better protect sensitive and classified information. Jeff is the author of many books including: *How to Get U.S. Government Contracts and Classified Work, Insider's Guide to Security Clearances, The Side Job Tool Box* and several novels.

Contact Jeff:
editor@redbikepublishing.com
Hear Jeff's Podcast at:
https://www.redbikepublishing.com/dodsecure

If you want an in-depth review of NISPOM(section by section) there is a NISPOM Fundamentals and ISP Cert training available at:
https://bennettinstitute.com.

Red Bike Publishing

Our company is registered as a government contractor company with the CCR and VetBiz (DUNS 826859691). Specifically we are a Service Disabled Veteran Owned Small Business. Red Bike Publishing provides high quality books and training @
www.redbikepublishing.com.

Additional Resources:

An additional study resource includes the *Self Inspection Handbook For NISP Contractors* available at the DCSA website and at Red Bike Publishing https://www.redbikepublishing.com

Searchable 32 CFR Part 117 available here: *https://www.redbikepublishing.com/ispcert/*

Books

This book, other security and NISP books and training are also available at our website. Helpful books include those part of the Security Clearances and Cleared Defense Contractor series by Red Bike Publishing:

- Insider's Guide to Security Clearances
- How to Get U.S. Government Contracts and Classified Work
- National Industrial Security Program Operating Manual (NISPOM)
- Self Inspection Guidebook for NISP Contractors
- International Traffic In Arms Regulation (ITAR)

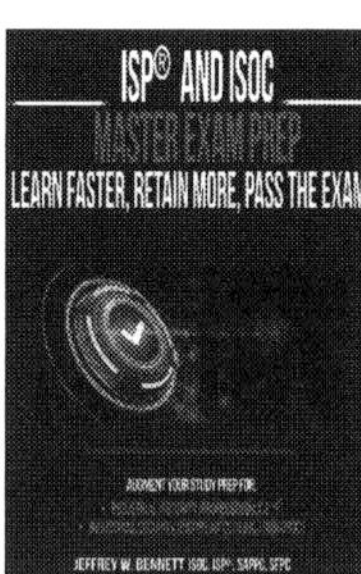

Training

Training topics include the follow either stand alone or as an FSO Certification Bundle https://www.redbikepublishing.com/fsocertification/:

- SF-312 Non Disclosure Briefing
- Insider Threat Training
- Derivative Classifier Training
- Security Awareness Training

Bennett Institute https://www.bennettinstitute.com

NISPOM Fundamentals Course-Training that discusses each chapter of the NISPOM in depth; more than 8 hours of recorded training

- Alternatively, you can take course one chapter or topic at a time
- Great study material. Each course provides completion certificates that can be used to earn CEUs for recertification.
- We also have a complimentary course available called Certification Test Tips

A special word of thanks and a favor to ask

Thank you for buying my book. I really appreciate you being a reader and hope you find it helpful. If you have any questions, please feel free to contact me.

I would really love to hear your feedback and your input would help to make the next version of this book and my future books better. Please leave a helpful review, where you purchased your book, of what you thought of it.

I would also ask that you let a friend know about the book as well. Thanks so much and best of success to you!!

Jeffrey W. Bennett

Sign up for our reader newsletter:
https://www.redbikepublishing.com/contact

For more information on cleared defense contracting, security clearances, and training, check out our video.
https://www.redbikepublishing.com/security/

Made in the USA
Middletown, DE
21 September 2023